Joe Stahlkuppe

Poodl

D0371009

Everything About Purchase, Care, Nutrition, Behavior, and Training

Filled with Full-color Photographs

Illustrations by Michele Earle-Bridges

BARRON'S

CONTENTS

3

POODLES: AN INTRODUCTION

The Poodle is a contrast between commonly held ideas and attitudes about the breed and the truth about the real dog. The unknowing see only a fancy dog with an unusual haircut. Genuine Poodle people know the tough, yet elegant, dog that excels as a true canine companion.

Everyone knows the "French" Poodle, don't they? Not necessarily! One of the most popular breeds in the world, the Poodle has often been cursed by the misconceptions such popularity can bring. People have neatly filed the concept of "Poodle" into classifications of superfluous, dandified, even useless as a *real* dog. This is far from the truth!

Origin of the Name

The Poodle is the national dog of France, but the breed isn't actually French. The dogs we know as Poodles (which the French call *caniches*) derive from early German retrievers

Poodles are among the most attractive and elegant breeds in the dog world. Their appearance sometimes obscures the fact that they are also among the most athletic and intelligent of dog breeds.

that came to be called *pudels*, or "puddlers," from the German verb *puddeln*, "to splash in or into water." Caniche, the French name for their adopted favorite, comes from the word *canard*, meaning duck. This made the caniche a "duck dog." Thus, in both their home country and in their adoptive land, Poodles are known, by name, for their ability to retrieve downed ducks or geese for hunters.

The Poodle Clip

This early Poodle was a stockier version of the standard or large Poodle of today. What many experts believe was a fortunate genetic mutation gave these tough retrievers a dense and tightly curled coat that made cold-water retrieving less chilling. Even the haircuts or clips that have contributed so much to the impression of the Poodle as a dandy, or a pampered pet, originated with hunters. Even before

POODLE POINT

To learn more about the physical appearance of Poodles take a look at the American Kennel Club's *Standard for the Poodle.*

the 1300s duck hunters began trimming away some of the Poodle's heavy coat to assist the dog in swimming after downed waterfowl in rough water. Thus, the easily recognized "lion clip," which left the Poodle with a full mane in front and shaved hindquarters, began as an effort by duck and goose hunters to cover the areas of the retrieving Poodle that would be most sensitive to cold while freeing up the rear of the dog to aid it in swimming. The puffs of hair left on the legs were not decoration but insulation to protect the dogs' joints from cold water. The oft-ridiculed pompon on the dog's three-quarter-length tail was left to serve as a type of rudder. It also made a useful signal flag

Poodle clips weren't always for decorative purposes. Originally, retrieving Poodles were trimmed to better help them swim. Joints and chest were left untrimmed to insulate them from the effects of icy-cold water.

that let hunters know the location of their dogs in choppy, rolling waters.

Poodle Functions

The Poodle is one of the oldest distinct dog breeds. Greek carvings from the first century A.D. depicted dogs that greatly resemble Poodles. European artwork and texts from the fifteenth century clearly show and describe Poodles in a variety of settings, from a working "water dog" to a popular pet.

Hunters and Retrievers

As retrievers, early Poodles spent a lot of time with humans. Hunting was a very serious endeavor that brought needed food to the table. Lost waterfowl were regarded as a great waste. Not only did Poodles need to be obedient to the hunters' commands, these dogs also had to be "soft-mouthed" so that they would not tear or bruise the flesh of the ducks or geese they retrieved. Poodles also had to be tough enough to bring in a large duck or goose that was only wounded and that still could put up quite a fight.

Poodles had to be patient as they waited, hidden, with their owners. They had to remain motionless so they would not frighten away incoming waterfowl. They had to stay in place until the command to go after their owners' kills was given. Sometimes a Poodle would be required to swim long distances, against the current, in turbulent water, towing one or more ducks or a large goose. Obedience, especially to shouted commands and hand signals, was a must.

The Poodle could not be quarrelsome with other hunters' retrievers, but it had to be strong enough and have sufficient endurance to make repeated retrieves before accompanying its

While appearing dandified, the Continental Poodle cut was originally based on the breed's use as a retriever.

master on the long walk home. These hardworking Poodles had to be able to survive on the sometimes meager fare they shared with their owners. Unlike hounds and other types of hunting dogs that were kept, often in kennels, for the chase or to attack and bring down game, Poodles usually became beloved domestic pets and actually lived with the hunter and his family.

Companions

Poodles served as nursemaids for toddlers, family watchdogs and protectors, and sturdy companions. Sometimes the Poodle would have to pull a cart to market for the hunter's wife. Some Poodles helped herd cattle. Poodles had to be courageous enough to battle predators intent on killing livestock. Poodles, which later would be viewed by some as soft pet dogs, handled all these chores and more.

Beginning as early as the thirteenth century in Germany, France, and other parts of Europe, the Poodle was recognized as the ideal combination of a hunter/worker and family dog. The long years of closeness to humankind Poodles have enjoyed (and their owners' subsequent selective breeding of the smartest, most obedient, and best retrievers) made an indelible mark on the form, structure, and personality of this breed.

Adaptability

During the many years it served as a companion and helpmate to humans, the Poodle adjusted and adapted to people, filling new and vastly different roles.

Gradually, beginning in the thirteenth or fourteenth century, Poodles came to be treasured by more than hunters and their families. The dogs' qualities as pets and their unique appearance began to attract people other than hunters, including wealthy Europeans and even royalty. Thanks to their newly elevated status, Poodles then moved from the modest, rural homes of waterfowlers to city houses and castles.

By the 1600s Poodles had become regular fixtures in portraits of landed gentry, wealthy merchants, and various royal families. To fit the needs of their new masters and mistresses, the dogs had to be bred to a desirable size. This was accomplished mainly by breeding a standard-size Poodle with smaller and smaller ones. Decreasing Poodle size soon became a major dog-breeding goal. The Miniature Poodle and early Toy Poodle clearly were already known by 1600. The Standard Poodle continued bringing in waterfowl, but even this largest member of the breed was becoming more popular as a showy pet.

Miniature Poodles, smaller than Standards and larger than Toys, still have a lot of Poodle glee and agility. Standards, Miniatures, and Toys are all judged by the same breed requirements, differing only in their respective sizes.

During the late fourteenth and fifteenth centuries Poodles became popular as performers in the traveling shows, circuses, and carnivals that provided much of the entertainment of that era. This role, one that continues today, helped Poodles become widespread over much of Europe and the British Isles. Capable and bright, seemingly pleased by the attention and applause, Poodles learned a wide range of tricks and routines that amazed and amused audiences.

Beautiful and Elegant

The Poodle is more than a mop of curly hair perched on the arm of some socialite or mincing along a boulevard at the end of a leash. The Poodle is more than a clever performer or statuesque show dog. Most Poodles still have the athletic build of their retriever ancestors. In very harmonious terms, the Poodle has long legs attached to a short body with a broad, full chest. The head of the Poodle is well-shaped and placed atop a fine yet muscular neck. Seen without the solid-colored, tight, curly coat, the Standard Poodle would physically resemble a number of other working bird dogs or water spaniels.

Sizes

The Standard Poodle, shorn of coat, is actually about the size and overall shape of such Continental hunting dogs as the Weimaraner, the German Shorthaired Pointer, or the Vizsla. The Standard Poodle of today is more than 15 inches (38.1 cm) in height at the shoulder (and is generally well above this limit). The Miniature Poodle is under 15 inches but above 10 inches (25.4 cm) in height at the shoulder. The height, at the shoulder, of a Toy Poodle must be 10 inches or below.

Coat

The Poodle's coat attracted the eye of the dog owner and the dog fancier who fashioned the dog's natural outerwear by trimming it, clipping it, plucking it, shaping it, and even dyeing it into a number of dramatic outlines and appearances.

Another variation, the corded Poodle, whose uncut coat falls in ropelike spirals instead of tight curls, never was as popular in the United States as it has been in other parts of the world.

The Real Dog Inside the Poodle

The Poodle has been relegated by some to the unfortunate status of a living, breathing fashion accessory. This attitude does both the dog and the dog's owner a real disservice. The Poodle, even in its toy variety, is much more than an adornment or an ornament. An ornament can be taken off and put away when not in use, but a dog needs consistent care, affection, and attention each and every day.

The Poodle owner suffers most when he or she fails to really know the dog for the versatile creature it can be. A person who purchases a Poodle solely for the visual impact the dog will have on passersby is getting a pet, and especially a Poodle, for all the wrong reasons! The Poodle is a very devoted and trusting canine whose pet qualities do not begin and end with its appearance.

This cream Standard Poodle amply shows off the beauty and refinement of the breed.

Disposition

Well-bred Poodles are usually happy, confident dogs. Poodles have been associated with humans long enough to fit in well in almost every kind of lifestyle. The Standard Poodle can grace a stroll with its owner in a city park, patrol a suburban backyard, or function in a duck blind. The Miniature Poodle can be a child's best friend, a family's furriest member, or a hardworking obedience trial dog. While equally at home in suburban or rural settings, the Toy Poodle can be just the right dog for an individual or couple bound by space constraints

POODLE POINT

Poodles owe their good dispositions to centuries of having been bred to be around humans.

Advice for Potential Poodle Owners

1. Be absolutely certain that you want to own a Poodle. Treat the purchase of a Poodle as an investment, a labor-intensive, time-consuming investment that will pay off only in direct proportion to the amount of hard, smart work you put into it. The Poodle coat alone will require a good deal of time and work to keep your potential pet looking good and feeling well. Invest only in a healthy Poodle from breeding stock known to be as free from inherited diseases and defects as possible, and that has test results to prove it.

2. Go places where quality Poodles are. Visit as many dog shows as you can. Sit back and watch how the judge decides which Poodle wins. Try to understand what makes one Poodle better than another. Try to gain the mental image of what a good Poodle should look like.

3. Don't fail to check out animal shelters and Poodle rescue organizations that might have just the right pet for you.

4. Find yourself a Poodle mentor, a respected breeder, exhibitor, or Poodle rescue person who will commit to be your teacher, advisor, and friend.

5. Find a Poodle-knowledgeable local veterinarian to advise you about Poodles and their health management.

in a small apartment, or for a retiree needing companionship. Poodles star as therapy dogs, bringing smiles to sick children, happiness to disabled older persons, and unreserved affection to the developmentally disadvantaged. The Poodle has proven many times over that a friendly dog can be medicine of a very special kind.

Intelligence

Poodles are quick to learn and slow to forget. A Poodle owner must learn to be consistent with his or her dog. A Poodle that has been allowed on the couch at one time will not understand being banned from that same couch later. Some Poodles react to such inequities with resentment.

Poodles, like their circus-dog ancestors, are usually easy to teach both commands and tricks. They learn from a variety of teachers and learning situations.

The Perfect Dog?

Is the Poodle the perfect breed? Of course not! The Poodle, as a breed with three varieties, is beset by some of the most serious genetic health problems in purebred dogs. There are great Poodles, but they don't come from casual sources (mass puppy-breeding facilities or haphazard backyard matings) and they don't come cheap or without responsibilities.

Each size of Poodle has its own special needs and issues. Standard Poodles are large dogs with all of the concerns that go along with active, bigger dogs. Whether clipped for a dog show or in a more utilitarian style, the Standard Poodle is still a big dog and must be treated as such. Standard Poodles are probably the most adaptable of the three Poodle sizes.

Miniature Poodles can often be dedicated to one person. This penchant for being a "one-person dog" is one reason minis often excel in obedience work. Miniature Poodles should always be safeguarded from situations where their "bigger than I really am" attitude could get them into trouble.

While the Standard and Miniature Poodles are members of the American Kennel Club's

Non-Sporting Breeds group, the Toy Poodle is a member of the AKC's Toy group. The smallest Poodle has become a very popular pet, an able competitor in the show ring, and no disgrace to its larger Poodle kin in achieving obedience titles. Toy Poodles, in the opinion of one breed expert, are somewhat like cats: "They can take you or leave you." Small the Toy Poodle may be, but it still shares much of the versatility and adaptability of the Standard and the Miniature.

Both the Standard Poodle and the Miniature Poodle are much older varieties than the Toy Poodle of today. Much of the knowledge and skill that went into developing and improving the bigger sizes definitely helped to create and establish the modern Toy Poodle.

Even though Poodles under 10 inches (25.4 cm) have been known for centuries, the Toy Poodle we have now is really a creation of recent decades. Toy Poodles, prior to the 1920s, were usually quite inferior to the Standards and Miniatures in quality and consistency. American Poodle breeders, working with some excellent Miniatures, gradually produced a Toy Poodle of much better quality than the odd-looking assortment of so-called toys of earlier years. Achieving small size without sacrificing the unique attributes of the true Poodle, a group of dedicated breeders literally made the Toy Poodle a smaller image of the stately Standard and the popular Miniature.

Drawbacks to Poodles

Poodles in all three sizes will have their lives controlled in part by the breed's most visibly obvious, outward characteristic: their coat. In every situation the curly Poodle coat must be considered. An ungroomed Poodle is very different from an ungroomed Cocker Spaniel,

The Toy Poodle shows the same love of life and joyful disposition seen in the Standard and Miniatures. These three Poodles add their own measure of mischief to the breed.

ungroomed Schnauzer, or even an ungroomed Beagle. Without regular attention, a Poodle's curly coat can become unsightly, unpleasant to be around, and even unhealthy.

Poodles also suffer some of the drawbacks that often come with being popular over a long span of time. There are more potential health problems involving the Poodle than plague many other breeds. A Poodle must be purchased from a reputable, knowledgeable source to increase the odds on getting a quality, healthy pet.

Because of the Poodle's intelligence, owners must become competent and consistent dog trainers. Poodles absolutely cannot be sometime pets relegated mainly to the backyard; they must be allowed to share in the lives of their humans.

UNDERSTANDING THE POODLE

The curly-coated dog edged closer to his duck hunting owner in a chilly duck blind in 15th-century France. Another dog, with the same distinctive coat snuggled near her owner on the couch in a 21st-century suburban American home. Both dogs are Poodles demonstrating the breed's great desire to be as close as possible to their humans.

Characteristic Poodle Behavior

Poodles have become the breed they are because of their nearness to humans for so many hundreds of years. Retriever, courtier, circus performer, or just a pet, the Poodle made its way with its intelligence, personality, and sociability. Poodles in any of the three sizes usually become devoted companions.

Most dogs need to be fed, watered, and walked at the same time every day. Poodles, adaptable though they are, may need routine in their lives a little more than some other breeds do. A person whose life is based on a muddled, disorganized, or "catch-as-catch-can"

Poodles are extremely versatile; they have served as circus performers, truffle-hunters, waterfowl retrievers, war-dogs, and, of course, family pets.

format is probably not the best owner for a Poodle. Poodles need consistency in their lives.

Perhaps the key behavioral characteristic of the Poodle is the breed's innate desire to please its owner. This gives Poodle owners an added responsibility in helping the dog know just what is expected of it. Unless the human is clear about what behaviors are satisfactory and which are not, how can the dog possibly know?

Poodles need a lot of affection, attention, and care. Problems with Poodles occur when any of these three ingredients is missing. A Poodle cannot know that an owner didn't give it a pat because he or she had a bad day at the office. The dog only knows it didn't get the customary sign of affection. A Poodle that can't get your attention in a positive way is much like a child in discovering a less than positive way to catch your eye. It is also true that although Poodles are tougher than their detractors will admit, they do need quality care to be quality pets.

Exuding the happy brightness of the Poodle breed, this chocolate Standard Poodle also looks ready to take on whatever adventure may come his way.

Poodles as Pets

There can be no better pet than a dog from a breed that has been chosen for its pet qualities for several hundred years. Poodles have a heritage in which their companion qualities transformed them from sporting dogs to pets. When a Poodle comes from a good genetic background, receives good care, and is well trained, a quality pet is usually the final result.

Poodles as Show Dogs

If the dog show hadn't been in existence when the Poodle came along, someone would have had to invent it. Poodles, perhaps even to

their detriment, have become among the showiest of dog breeds. Watching a perfectly groomed Poodle move smoothly around a show ring is the picture in many people's minds when dog shows are mentioned.

Poodles in Obedience Work

The Poodle excels in the show ring in part because of the combined arts of dog breeding and dog grooming. Poodles do well in obedience due to a combination of the skills of breeding and training. Poodles add much dash and charm to show-ring competitions, but it is in obedience that the blending of two innate Poodle characteristics really shines: the breed's exceptional intelligence and deep, abiding desire to please its owner. When you have a bright dog you are blessed. When you have a bright, motivated dog, you are twice blessed!

Poodles are among the top performers in obedience and agility trials.

Poodles have done exceedingly well in obedience trials ever since these kinds of competitions began, in both Europe and the United States. Obedience trials, like those sanctioned by the American Kennel Club, allow dogs and owners to pursue a number of obedience titles; among them are Companion Dog (CD); Companion Dog Excellent (CDX); Utility Dog (UD); and Utility Dog Excellent (UDX). Each of these obedience titles, and several other advanced and specialized degrees, is an acknowledgment that both dog and trainer have worked hard on an increasingly difficult set of commands performed under varying conditions.

Part of Poodle ownership means at least considering obedience training and trials if the dog shows any promise in that direction. Obedience trials are usually held in conjunction with dog shows. Skilled obedience judges conduct the trials and grade each dog on its performance in following its owner's commands. Obedience work isn't easy, but most Poodle owners who undertake it consider it very rewarding and well worth the effort!

Poodles as Retrievers

Modern Poodles certainly don't threaten to replace the Labrador Retriever as the most popular breed used in hunting and in retriever trials. However, some Poodles do still serve in their ancient role and continue to perform it well.

The stylish Poodle of today got its start in the bays, rivers, and marshes of Europe as the best waterfowl retriever of its time.

Even in the modern retriever breeds, some dogs simply don't do as well as others. Generally, if you want a working retriever of any breed, seek a dog that has a number of actual retrievers in its close family background.

Other Poodle Contributions

Poodle fans are generally an adventurous lot. They have been willing to demonstrate the versatility of their breed in as many venues as possible. Poodle teams have pulled dogsleds in competitions with northern breeds like Malamutes and Huskies. Poodles have been taught to herd livestock. Poodles have served as war dogs. Poodles have gone along with trailing hounds in search of game. Poodles have been guide dogs for the sight-impaired and therapy dogs. John Steinbeck's Standard Poodle, Charley, traveled all across the United States with his Pulitzer Prize–winning owner.

POODLE POINT

To be at its best a Poodle must live in close proximity to human beings.

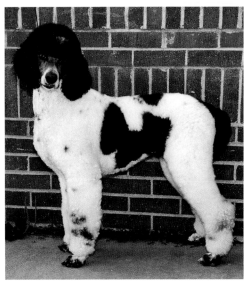

While not as exotic as the Labradoodle and some of the other "poo" types, this spotted or parti-colored Poodle shows coloration not accepted by the American Kennel Club, but which is acceptable in some other countries and in some other registries.

A Poodle's coat gives a good indication of the overall quality of the dog's breeding, feeding, and medical care.

Poodles as "Designer" Dogs

Some breeders have crossed the Poodle with other kinds of dogs. Most people have heard of these dogs of mixed-Poodle ancestry but may not recognize them for what they are—hybrids or mongrels! These crossbreeds are often given clever designations like "cock-a-poos," "peke-a-poos," and so forth and have been widely sold as pets. They may sometimes be good pets but they are not, in *any* way, purebred, and as such, each "something-a-poo" certainly should be spayed or neutered! One of the most interesting crosses involves the blending of the Poodle with the Labrador Retriever. This cross, referred to as the "Labradoodle" (there is also a cross with the

Golden Retriever—the "Goldendoodle"—and literally dozens of other Poodle crossbreeds), was made to put the Poodle's curly, nonshed coat on a stockier body to serve as a guide dog for the sight-impaired. Early reports state that Poodle-Lab mixtures have performed well in this role.

> ## POODLE POINT
>
> Poodles have been crossed with a number of dog breeds. Despite their high price tags, these "designer dogs" are in fact simply mixed breed dogs.

Poodles are usually excellent mothers and imbue their offspring with many of the early lessons that all dogs need to know. Pay close attention to the mother of any puppy you are considering, for she often determines much of what her puppies will become.

SHARING YOUR HOME WITH A POODLE

Some breeds of dogs seem content to be animal afterthoughts or simply pets. Poodles only do well when they are full partners in a home and family. Some breeds may survive when relegated to a dog house in the backyard. Such treatment would break a Poodle's heart.

Choosing to bring a Poodle into your life may require you to make some lifestyle modifications. You may not be able to take spur-of-the-moment trips because you must consider your dog. Entertaining guests in your home may mean arranging for the safety and comfort of your dog. Housekeeping chores that you might have neglected for yourself must be done to avoid compounding the work when a curious Poodle gets into a half-eaten pizza left on the coffee table. Adding a Poodle to your life is more than just getting a dog to keep in the backyard. Poodles are companion pets. They need closeness with their humans to complete their lives.

Poodles are ready to give their lives for their owners. All they ask in return are safe and comfortable environments and loads of attention and love.

The Poodle's Coat

Whether your Poodle is a tiny Toy, an active Miniature, or a robust Standard, one factor is a constant: the dog's coat. The Poodle coat, the breed's trademark, should be the same for all three sizes. A Poodle's coat is dense and curly and will require regular brushing and grooming to look its best. Brushing will be your job and can take a couple of hours per week or more. Grooming is often best left to professional dog groomers whose expertise in trimming, shaping, and washing is well worth whatever it costs.

The Poodle's coat does have a strong positive—it does not shed like the coats of other canines. This one element accounts for much of the Poodle's popularity with people who have allergies. The Poodle's coat may require a lot of care, but it doesn't contribute to airborne particles like the hair of most other dog breeds.

Poodles do particularly well in multi-dog homes as long as each Poodle is given some special individualized attention.

Smart Dogs Need Smart Owners

One of the main reasons the Poodle isn't the right dog for every individual or every family centers on the breed's basic intelligence. Poodles have lived in close quarters with human beings for hundreds of years. Because humans tend not to suffer stupid dogs under these circumstances, a type of intense selection for intelligence took place.

Owning a Poodle is different from owning a mixed breed or a dog of some other breed. If you are to have a successful relationship with a smart Poodle, you must be a smart Poodle owner! You need to recognize that inconsistencies negatively affect smarter dogs more. To act one way one time and another way another time may confuse a Poodle and make it distrustful of you.

Poodles and Children

Poodles and children can have happy, lifelong relationships. Poodles are affectionate and devoted to their young masters and mistresses. Some children, on the other hand, are neglectful of and even cruel to animals. Cruel, unfair treatment could turn a loving, trusting Poodle into a distrusting and fearful pet.

Children should always be supervised when playing with a pet. Wise owners will take time to teach children the proper, caring, and acceptable way to treat a dog. When children

POODLE POINT

Young children should always be supervised when they are playing with pets, including Poodles.

Poodles are usually quite good with older owners. Good judgment should, however, be used when pairing a frail elderly person with a rambunctious young Standard Poodle. A Miniature or a Toy might be a better choice in some instances.

recognize that the Poodle is more than just an animated, plush, stuffed animal, they are more apt to gain a real understanding of how to act correctly around a pet.

Poodles and the Elderly

Poodles are excellent pets for people who have reached seniorhood. Poodles are loving, devoted, and willing companion animals. Many stories abound in Poodle lore about older people who had never had a dog before and became inseparable with their first Poodle. Lonely people can find great solace in the tender attentions of a well-behaved Poodle. Retirees whose lives sometimes lack the structure of their working years can find routine and order in the schedule that must be followed in caring for a Poodle. Brushing can keep older arms and hands supple. Walks with the Poodle are good exercise for dog and human alike.

Poodles and Other Pets

Poodles usually adapt well to other pet animals in a home setting. Although it is important to show all pets the necessary attention to stave off petty jealousies, Poodles aren't usually troublemakers.

For the owner who takes time, as gradually as possible, to introduce a new Poodle puppy into a household where cats live, the results can be very gratifying. Cats and Poodles can learn to coexist peacefully, and once they do they often become close pals. Human supervision to oversee the early interactions between pets can avoid most problems. Feeding two pets separately, at least for a while, is wise. Leaving a young Poodle alone with another pet is certainly unwise until the two have accepted each other.

Keep the Poodle a Real Dog

Poodles have a long and distinguished history of being *real* dogs in service to real people. Just because some people treat their Poodle like a canine Barbie doll doesn't negate the fact that the Poodle is a living creature with all that brings, good and bad. Acquire a Poodle to be an actual dog, not a plaything. The Poodle will suffer greatly if viewed as an object, and you will miss out by never getting to know all the joys that being a Poodle owner can bring. Avoid this combination of tragedies and keep your Poodle a *real* dog!

CARING FOR YOUR POODLE

There is no more dedicated pet and canine companion in all of dogdom than the Poodle. Such dedication deserves an owner both knowledgeable and concerned about the needs of the Poodle.

Housing a Poodle

Some breeds actually thrive on being outdoor dogs. This is not the case with the Poodle. That is not to say that Poodles don't enjoy being outside; they do. However, Poodles are more human-oriented than some breeds and prefer to be around people.

It is possible for a Poodle to adjust to living in a doghouse in a suburban backyard, but that would be a sad fate. Poodles crave the companionship of human beings, especially their own human beings. To attempt to make a Poodle into an occasional pet is to engage in one of the cruelest forms of animal abuse. Don't buy a Poodle if you don't want it to be near you!

A Poodle should live with you in your home. A cage/crate/carrier will provide all your dog

The Standard Poodle is a dignified canine aristocrat concealing the soul of a buffoonish clown.

will need for those times when it must be absent from you. Indoors, with you, is the best place for a dog that adores you. For those brief and temporary times when your Poodle may need to be out of your home, a draft-free doghouse in a fenced backyard or kennel run is useful, but only when *absolutely* necessary.

The Poodle and Exercise

Exercise is an important element in any Poodle's life. Although a Poodle is quite content to stay by the side of your easy chair, long walks, jogs in the park, or hiking in the country will also be enjoyable, but only if you are along. If you want your Poodle to get enough exercise, you'll have to go as well. One dog expert stated, "There are dogs that will pull you along on a walk and dogs that will ignore you entirely, but the Poodle goes for the walk only because you are going for a walk, too!"

An active Poodle is a healthy Poodle. Exercise, regardless of the size of the dog, is a key element in the life of this onetime sporting breed.

POODLE POINT

Poodles need a lot of love, attention, and care, which is part of their special charm.

Standard Poodles are large, strong, and robust. Although they aren't usually as hyperactive as some breeds, they do enjoy running. They need consistency in their exercise to remain in good condition. Consistency will mean exercise every day, not every week or so! Some Poodle

Poodles, like these youngsters, must depend on their owners for the kind of care that will keep them safe and comfortable. Poodle ownership is a wonderful experience but carries with it some responsibilities to ensure the well-being of the dog.

owners who don't enjoy running alongside their dogs get long leashes, especially those on a handheld reel. These owners keep their dogs on leash and let the dogs circle them at whatever pace and at whatever distance (up to the end of the leash) the dog chooses.

Less than Obvious Needs

Caring for your Poodle clearly means providing the dog with a good home, good food, good training, and a safe environment. But to flourish, Poodles do need more than these obvious requirements. They need your affection, your attention, and your good judgment to make their lives happy.

Love Loving your Poodle may seem to be an easy obligation to fulfill, yet many people fail at it miserably. It is not enough to love an adorable Poodle puppy; you must love the dog when it is an awkward adolescent, and even more when it is an aging senior. You must love the dog when it does things that make you proud as well as when it does things that embarrass you or cost you money.

Attention Like other members of your household, your Poodle will need its share of your time every day. Giving your pooch a cursory pat on the head when you come in tired from your job may not seem like much to you. To your Poodle, however, your attention—even if it's simply the touch of your hand—is an absolutely thrilling reward. A kind word and a little playtime are prizes of great worth to your Poodle.

If you are too busy to give your Poodle the daily attention it needs to thrive, then you are too busy to own this or any other dog. Factor into your schedule the time you need to spend with your pet. If you can't give this caring dog

Car travel for a Poodle is best and most safely done in a carrier or with the dog fastened in a canine seat belt.

at least an hour a day, then wait until you can before you buy a Poodle.

Good Judgment

Your Poodle will depend on you to make the decisions that affect its life. Use good judgment when addressing such issues as those described here:
• Don't give your Poodle table scraps that could lead to obesity and other health problems.
• Don't let your Poodle ride unrestrained in your car.
• Don't let small children, or unruly older children, hurt your Poodle with rough and careless play. Always supervise them.
• Don't let a Poodle go without regular grooming.
• Always visit the veterinarian with your dog at least two times each year.
• Remember that your Poodle is a living, breathing investment, and protect this investment in every way possible!

Traveling by Car

A Poodle's nearness to its human family will often involve the dog in many short car trips. Longer trips, however, require planning and preparation. In either case, don't be careless just because your Poodle is often a passenger in your automobile.

As fine a companion as your Poodle may be, it is still just a dog. You can't expect any dog to understand, avoid, and overcome all the physical hazards that can befall a pet in unknown territory. If you allow your Poodle to stray away, even for just one moment, that could be the last time you will see your dog alive! Be cautious; keep your Poodle with you and safe. Whether you and your dog are taking a trip across town or across the country, there are some good, commonsense rules to follow:

• Always have your Poodle ride in its carrier whenever it goes somewhere with you in an automobile. A second choice would be to fasten the Poodle into a canine safety belt or harness. Never let your pet ride in a vehicle unrestrained.

• Poodles, especially smaller ones, can't go for long periods without eating. Bring some of your pet's favorite foods with you and use them moderately at travel breaks on longer trips.

• If your trip is several hours long, stop every hour or so to allow your pet to have some on-leash and well-supervised exercise and a relief break.

When traveling in an automobile, a pet should always ride in its carrier to avoid injuries that could come from being tossed around the car in the event of sudden stops, sharp turns, or accidents.

When it is not in the Poodle's best interest to accompany an owner on a trip, boarding the pet can be a good alternative.

• Never leave your Poodle in a parked car unless you leave the motor running and the air conditioner on! Any day when the temperature reaches as high as 60°F (15.6°C) can turn your parked car, even with the windows partially down, into an automotive version of a solar oven (see "Heatstroke," page 87).

• Always carefully prepare for any overnight trips. Check with auto clubs, travel guides, and the long-distance reservation numbers of hotel/motel chains to be certain that your well-behaved Poodle will be a welcomed guest in your room. Never try to slip a pet into a lodging place that you know doesn't permit pets. That is illegal, and also further prejudices innkeepers against allowing pet guests.

Traveling by Air

Traveling by air with a pet has become much more complicated and fraught with difficulties in recent years. Some airlines no longer allow any

A POODLE

pets to be brought on the plane as carry-on luggage. Cargo holds often are not the safest or most comfortable locations for family pets. As a part of the new reality concerning airline travel, make flying with your pet the exception rather than the rule.

Boarding Your Poodle

There are trips that may not lend themselves to having your Poodle accompany you. Some circumstances make a long trip with your dog impossible. If you can't take your Poodle with you, one of your options is to board your dog. While being away from your Poodle may be somewhat traumatic for both of you, boarding can be a very good option.

Boarding kennels have become much more numerous and much more professionally managed than they were some decades ago. Most boarding kennel owners and managers are dog people themselves and take excellent care of their lodgers. The American Boarding Kennel Association has a list of accredited kennels in your area. Write or phone the ABKA for further information (see "Useful Addresses and Literature," page 93).

You may be able to leave your pet at home while you travel if you have a trusted relative, friend, or neighbor who can provide in-home care. This is a very good solution for many dogs.

In a similar manner, pet sitters are now available in most parts of the country. These licensed and bonded individuals are able to handle your dog's care in a loving and skillful

Always watch your Poodle being loaded on the same flight that you are to take. Be courteous and polite, but insist!

manner. Always ask for references and then check them before you leave on your trip.

Many veterinarians handle boarding for their regular patients (which is what your Poodle should be). Because your Poodle is already known at the veterinary clinic, your absence may be less stressful.

When traveling with your Poodle, make every effort to keep it safe and comfortable.

Poodles travel well, if their owners have thoroughly planned and anticipated their needs and comfort.

BEFORE YOU GET A POODLE

Ownership of any dog should be a carefully considered decision. Owning such a human-oriented dog as the Poodle requires all the more forethought and planning.

Poodles are beautiful. Poodles are stylish. Poodles are smart. Poodles attract attention. But none of these reasons is the *right* one to own a Poodle. Some people want to be seen walking down the street with a perfectly groomed Poodle, the dog serving simply as a status symbol. But using a canine in this context is certainly not a good reason to own any dog.

The *right* reason to own a Poodle is to have a companion that will share your life. Anyone who wants a sometime plaything should choose a stuffed animal and leave all living dogs alone.

This apricot Poodle is only six months old, yet he already has the charisma of a much older dog. He amply shows that from Standards to Miniatures to Toys, Poodles are all the same except for size. This one is a Toy.

Making the Right Decision

Some things you should factor into your decision to acquire a Poodle are:

1. Is each person in your home really aware of what owning a Poodle will entail?

2. Has each person agreed to help care for this Poodle and help it develop as it should?

3. Will each family member take time every day to show the dog affection and attention?

4. Is your family ready to make the financial investment a Poodle may require (perhaps several hundred dollars in initial cost), including all the expenses for food, grooming (if done by a professional), and veterinary care?

5. Is each person in your home willing to make every effort to keep the Poodle safe and comfortable?

6. Is there one specific, responsible person who can spend a substantial amount of time at home to help a new Poodle pet settle in?

Choosing a Poodle puppy is always an enjoyable experience. Doing everything to help that puppy grow into a well-behaved adult isn't always fun, but it certainly is worth it!

These questions shouldn't be answered casually. If your family can't do these things faithfully, you should wait before acquiring a Poodle. Save yourself some heartache (and an innocent Poodle from a false start) by being mature enough, and unselfish enough, to put off what may not be a good idea right now.

Toy, Miniature, or Standard?

Few breeds can give you the size options you have with the Poodle. The standards for the breed stress that the three varieties should be identical except for size. The size decision can be based purely on your preferences. You should know that height, not weight, is the deciding factor in designating a Poodle as a Standard, Miniature, or Toy. It is possible that

a chunky Toy Poodle could actually weigh more than a thin Miniature. Weight is not even mentioned in the AKC Poodle standard.

Toys: The Toy Poodle, under 10 inches (25.4 cm) in height at the shoulder, has gained much popularity in recent years. While Toys are obviously smaller than Standards and Miniatures, they should still be all Poodle—that is, purebred. Cute as they are, thanks to their diminutive size, Toys aren't always the best choice when very small children are in a home. These little dogs are sometimes quite vocal, but they have the same love and devotion for their owners all Poodles possess. There are very tiny Toy Poodles labeled "Teacup Poodles." Teacups have been produced by breeding together increasingly small dogs. One respected Poodle breeder sheds light on these tiny dogs by stating that Teacups affect their owners in two ways: (1) in the pocketbook, from all the added health expenses; (2) in the heart, from having to watch the dog suffer from abnormalities and inherited illnesses until it finally dies a very early death.

Miniatures: Miniature Poodles, the most popular of the three sizes, fit that special niche for those who want a dog that is between a small Toy Poodle and the strapping Standard. Many Miniatures feature the best aspects of both the other sizes and have these qualities in a tidy, but not tiny, package. Miniatures are over 10 inches (25.4 cm) but less than

Miniature Poodles are sprightly and always ready for fun. They are gregarious and enjoy playing with other companions, canine or human.

Standard Poodles are not classified as small dogs. They are in the Doberman, Airedale Terrier, size range and need consistent and regular exercise to burn off energy and keep trim.

15 inches (38.1 cm) in height, measured at the dog's shoulder. Regardless of what a Poodle's papers may say, if it is over this height limit the dog is a Standard. A Poodle under 10 inches in height is a Toy.

Standards: Standard Poodles are over 15 inches (38.1 cm) in height, and are often quite a few inches taller. Standards are good pets for people who prefer a larger dog. Like the Miniature and the Toy, the Standard retains all the best Poodle characteristics. This largest variety still has the playfulness of its smaller counterparts, but blends it with a certain dignity.

A Standard Poodle requires more room and exercise than its smaller kin. Both the Miniature and the Toy have surged ahead of the bigger Poodle in popularity. This may stem from the added requirements that larger dogs bring to a modern dog owner. Higher fences, stronger gates, more items to put up out of Pierre's way are all additional considerations for those who prefer a standard. These big Poodles can be effective deterrents to unwanted visitors. They also often show a seriousness of demeanor that makes even some youngsters seem wise beyond their years.

Faddish animals called "royal" or "imperial" Standard Poodles are merely larger than usual

Poodle puppies are adorable, but then so are adult Poodles. Some of the best Poodle pets available may well be rescued dogs in real need of new homes.

Standards and are not rarer or more valuable. This nomenclature is more a way to sell larger Poodles than it is a special category.

Puppy or Adult?

The devotion that most Poodles show for their previous owners could be a negative factor in acquiring an adult. It is tough for some dogs, even some Poodles, to adjust to a new owner. Evaluate adult Poodles that may be offered to you strictly on an individual basis. A puppy can be what you mold it to be. You may not know immediately if an adult can fit with you or you with it. On the plus side for obtaining an adult is that it will still need your love, care, and attention, but nowhere near the initial amount of time a puppy may demand.

If you want a Poodle, don't have time to devote to a puppy, and an adult (especially a rescued one) is available, try the older dog. Many Poodle fans began in just this fashion, several Poodles ago.

Rescued Poodles

There are many adults and puppies available as rescued dogs. Through no fault of their own, these Poodles don't have owners. In most cases they will make wonderful pets and companions. The Poodle Club of America, the PCA Poodle rescue organization, or other groups (see "Useful Addresses and Literature," page 93) may know of adult Poodles or puppies that need good homes. There may be a rescued Poodle that is just what you need and want.

Male or Female?

Poodles of either sex can make excellent pets. Both males and females can do well in the hot competition of the show ring, and both have excelled in obedience work. The choice of the sex of your potential Poodle is largely one of personal preference. Male Poodles, even Toys, are generally "all male," but without the excessive "macho" behavior of some breeds. Female Poodles are, by definition, quite feminine, perhaps a bit more refined in appearance, and often a little smaller.

The choice of color is largely a cosmetic decision. Pick the best Poodle available, regardless of color, and you will never regret it. Fortunately there are lots of good Poodles in lots of sizes and lots of colors.

Unspayed female Poodles go into a three-week-long heat cycle about twice a year. The inconvenience of having to protect an unspayed female from amorous male dogs and the added bother of in-season discharge for a dog that stays indoors make owning an unspayed female a bit more challenging. Spaying a nonbreeding female solves both of these problems and a number of other health concerns as well.

Males have a tendency to "mark their territory" with urine. This isn't a problem outside in the backyard or at the relief spot, but an unhousebroken male (and some housebroken males) may carry this marking behavior indoors with him. Unneutered males are also preoccu-

pied with females that are in heat. You will have to be extra careful about not letting your Poodle escape from your supervision when a nearby female is in season.

Although spayed or neutered dogs cannot be shown in American Kennel Club conformation shows, they can exhibit their skills in obedience trials. Spaying or neutering is one of the very best things you can do for your Poodle.

What Color?

Poodles come in some of the most beautiful solid colors in all of dogdom. The blacks, whites, blues, browns, apricots, grays, creams, café-au-laits, silvers, and other accepted Poodle colors

This Poodle won Best-in-Show at the prestigious Westminster Dog Show. Chances are this classy dog is a very good representative of the breed as well.

Show Quality or Pet Quality?

Show dogs of all breeds, and especially of a popular and widely exhibited breed like the Poodle, are the products of generation after generation of carefully planned breeding. Thousands of Poodle breeders have diligently studied, worked, restudied, and reworked to produce the very best Poodles that have ever been bred. The success rates for producing top-quality Poodles are never very high. As a realistic saying among dog breeders asserts, "Great show dogs come in clusters—clusters of one!"

There is much more to exhibiting a Poodle than just cleaning Pierre up and taking him over to a dog show and claiming a blue ribbon. Your Poodle may be an excellent pet. It may also be a reasonably good representative of the breed, Toy, Miniature, or Standard. To you, your Poodle may look as good as any of the dogs in the Poodle books you've seen, and as good as any of the other Poodles at a dog show. Unfortunately, the decision of which dog wins isn't left up to you, because you aren't the judge!

To designate a pup as "show quality" is only an informed guess at best. Experienced Poodle experts might put such a label on a good-looking puppy from a well-bred litter, but it would still be just a guess.

"Pet quality" is in no way a slur on the health, the temperament, or the companion capacities of a young Poodle. This Poodle's ears may be set a bit too high. Its tail may be set a bit too low. There may be some cosmetic flaw that makes

all have their advocates. Blacks and whites are more popular for dog shows, but browns, grays, and even the apricots are often seen in the show ring. Poodles in nonstandard colors, such as parti-colored dogs, do exist and some have become excellent pets, but they cannot be shown in AKC events. Unless you absolutely must have a specific color, search for the best Poodle available. Choose quality of the total dog over a lesser dog of just the right color.

If your goal is the best possible pet and size, sex, and color aren't that important, the Poodle is the breed for you!

POODLE POINT

While Poodles are some of the greatest show dogs imaginable, they also make some of the very best pet dogs. Sometimes they can even be both!

this pup a loser as a potential show dog. That certainly doesn't mean it can't be a winner as your pet choice! Although eliminated from exhibition for some minor defect, this Poodle could have all the charm, intelligence, and devotion to make it the perfect pick for you!

If you do decide that dog showing seems like an intriguing pastime you might like to pursue, your options are wide open. Most dog shows are good places to meet people who can help you understand what is required in this fast-paced, highly competitive world. Even if you know that you want a Poodle only as a family pet, visit as many dog shows as possible to meet respected Poodle breeders who may be able to help you find the right Poodle for you.

If you have some special ambition for your Poodle, like using him as a retriever, look for the Poodle you are seeking from among families of dogs that have shown some abilities in this specific area. Otherwise, most Poodles will do well for the average pet owner.

Selecting a Puppy

Finding the right Poodle for you and your family will depend, at least in part, on what you are seeking. Regardless of what you are looking for, don't expect any breeder to sell you the top prospect of the year. This just won't happen, especially if you are a first-time Poodle owner. There are some things you can do to help you in your quest for the right Poodle:

✔ Study Poodles. The more you know, the easier your search will be. Talk to as many Poodle breeders as possible. Visit as many shows as you can. Contact the Poodle Club of America for breeders near you.

✔ Clearly define what you want in a Poodle. Decide what size will best fit your lifestyle. Think about what you will want a Poodle to do (family pet, obedience trials, perhaps retrieving). Decide if an adult dog would do as well as a puppy.

✔ Understand the possible pitfalls that can plague any dog buyer. Learn what paperwork

should accompany any purchased puppy. Fully understand all guarantees and rights before money changes hands.

✔ If showing your Poodle is something you are sincerely interested in, discuss with several top Poodle breeders the possibilities of becoming a part owner of a pup with show potential.

✔ Try to see the parents, or at the very least, the mother of any puppy you might be considering. You may see something of what your potential choice could look like, and act like,

---

POODLE POINT

The perfect Poodle for you may be as near as the closest Poodle rescue organization. Don't neglect the idea of adopting a rescued pet.

Poodle puppies, like these cuties, are always winners when they go to the right homes. Good pets are molded from basic Poodle material and the right home usually produces the right pet.

sorts of Poodle puppies are available to you. You may later decide to buy that first puppy you saw, but you should visit other litters to gain the proper perspective.

✔ Be sure to remember that the right Poodle puppy, or adult Poodle, for that matter, may be waiting for you at an animal shelter or at one of the Poodle rescue organizations. If a pet Poodle is your primary goal, don't ignore the chance to find the right pet and give a homeless Poodle a new start at the same time.

Your Poodle's Documentation

You can greatly increase your chances of getting the right registered Poodle puppy by making sure you get the proper paperwork that should accompany that puppy. You can go a long way toward getting a quality Poodle with all the right documentation by choosing the right Poodle breeder. Select a breeder with a good reputation for producing top-quality Poodles, along with proven track records in dog shows or obedience trials.

Before you purchase a Poodle puppy, you must be certain that the following documents are available:

✔ The pup's complete medication and worming records with all the correct dates.

✔ A health certificate, signed by the breeder's veterinarian, attesting that this puppy has been examined and is healthy.

as an adult. You may also observe the living conditions into which this puppy has been born.

✔ If there are several puppies that meet your general requirements as to sex, size, color, and overall quality, ask the breeder to separate these from any that aren't for sale or that don't fall into the categories you have predesignated. This will make your choice much simpler.

✔ Gently handle each puppy correctly, using both hands. Support its rear end and hind legs with one hand while steadying its chest with the other. Make certain that you closely supervise your children if they pick up any pups.

✔ Watch the puppies as they interact with their littermates. Observe the way the pups are around their mother. Reinforce your own learning about pack behavior (See "Pack Behavior," page 57) and the mother dog's way of maintaining control over her babies.

✔ Don't get all excited and pick the first puppy from the first litter you see. Arrange to see other litters to increase your awareness of what

✔ The pup's AKC registration application signed by both you and the breeder. This key document is what you must send in (on time!) to the American Kennel Club to make certain your Poodle is "registered." You can also give your pup its registered name on this application.

✔ The Poodle puppy's pedigree, showing its ancestry. (This document will be only as good as the puppy source you have picked.)

✔ A return agreement specifying that should your plans change and you can't keep the Poodle, it will be returned to the breeder rather than disposed of in another manner (sold, given away, euthanized, or turned over to an animal shelter). This is sometimes optional, but tells you a great deal about the quality of the breeder you have chosen.

✔ A spay or neuter agreement, for your signature, that assures the breeder that you will have this pet pup rendered incapable of reproducing. (This is also a good indicator that you have chosen a reputable breeder.)

If the documentation, other than the optional paperwork, isn't available, if there is a promise made to send these papers in the mail, don't buy this puppy at this time! Without the right documentation, for example, your Poodle may not be allowed in any AKC shows.

Christmas Puppies

At some point you may have seen, read about, or even been part of a cheery holiday scene with a joyful child getting a puppy for Christmas. This may seem heartwarming, but in cold reality, it is a bad idea. Your Poodle puppy deserves to be more than just one of several presents under a Christmas tree. Far too often Christmas puppies also come as a surprise to the child's parents, who may be ill-prepared for a living gift that requires a lot of care.

Puppies need to be the center of attention to feel welcome in their new homes. If you are contemplating giving a puppy as a present, give it after the busy holidays are over. You could give a book or DVD about Poodles and even an announcement that a puppy would be coming after Christmas. One sensible breeder supplies an intended puppy giver with a personalized DVD showing the newborn puppy, its mother, and its brothers and sisters. This DVD offers helpful hints on how to get ready for the puppy and how to treat it when it arrives. By taking this unique approach, this breeder found a way to make Christmas bright for a child without making the holiday confusing, perplexing, and frightening to the puppy.

Poodles should never be surprise gifts like at Christmas time. Owning a Poodle, especially a Poodle puppy or a rescued Poodle, should always be a carefully planned endeavor.

BRINGING YOUR POODLE HOME

Bringing a new Poodle puppy or even an adult Poodle into your home for the first time can be a traumatic experience for both you and the dog. It is also the first step in establishing the animal as a key part of your household. Be careful to make this first homecoming as free from stress as possible. Enjoy your new Poodle and give it a chance to learn to enjoy being with you.

Be Prepared

Preparing to share your home and life with a Poodle requires some serious commonsense thinking on the part of the prospective pet owner. All aspects of the home and lifestyle should be carefully evaluated (and possibly modified) to ensure the safety and comfort of the new Poodle.

The Cage/Crate/Carrier

One of the most important preparatory purchases for you to make is a cage/crate/carrier (see "Crate Training Your Poodle," page 62).

This young Miniature Poodle is at just about the right age to begin serious training. The pup is ready to learn how it can get the praise and treat rewards from his owner by doing what the owner wants.

There are several versions of these canine protection/containment products, which are generally lumped together under the single word "crate." This crate should not be perceived by you or any member of your family as a miniprison for solitary confinement for your new pet; the opposite is true.

Dogs, by nature, are denning animals. As such they have a great psychological yearning for a place within your environment that is uniquely theirs. An airline carrier, an enclosed crate designed for just this purpose, or one of the collapsible cages will fulfill this denning requirement. Make this first purchase well before you bring your pooch home. Your Poodle will do immeasurably better with such a manufactured den than without one. Choose a cage/crate/carrier for the adult size of the Poodle, not for the size it is as a puppy. You can always devise partitions to make the inside area the right current size for your new puppy as it grows.

Dishes/Bowls

Your Poodle puppy will need two sturdy, not easily tipped-over dishes or bowls—one for water, one for food. Due to the amount of wear and tear these items will take, purchase ones that have been designed for canine rather than human use. They should also be made of materials that can be placed in a dishwasher or, in the case of the food bowl, that are microwave-safe. There are even water bottles that can be affixed to the crate.

Your new puppy will need a number of things: a carrier, a lead, a regular collar, a training lead and collar, food and water dishes, grooming tools, some doggy toys, and the food it had been eating at its first home.

Food

Whether your new Poodle is an adult or a puppy, purchase some of the same food that the animal has been eating.

Collar and Leash

A good leash (often called a "lead") and an equally good collar are necessary for your new Poodle. This first collar is not the training collar (see "Training Equipment," page 64) you will need to teach your young Poodle; it is an everyday collar, and should be the right size for an active youngster who has not yet been leash trained. Regardless of which size Poodle you have, the collar should be snug, but able to slip over the dog's head with about one inch (2.5 cm) of clearance. Collars should always be checked often to see that they haven't become too tight for a rapidly growing young Poodle. This collar and an appropriate leash (depending on your Poodle's size) will allow safety and control of the puppy when you are out walking or whenever the pup is not inside your home or a fenced yard.

Grooming Equipment

Grooming equipment is necessary from the start to keep your young Poodle looking good. You will need a good bristle brush, a "slicker" brush, and a comb designed for grooming long-haired dogs (see "Grooming Tools," page 70).

While a backyard is always a plus, your Poodle should have her own place within your home. A cage, crate, or carrier gives your Poodle just such a place of her own.

Toys

Most Poodles need toys, both to play with and to "own." Just having some favorite play-things around for your Poodle will serve much the same purpose as a child's security blanket or favorite stuffed animal.

One way to help a puppy settle in a little better is to bring some favorite belonging (loaded with the scent of its mother and litter-mates) from the place where the pup was born.

The Trip Home

Riding in an automobile is nothing to you, but to an eight-week-old Poodle puppy it could be a terrifying experience. Aside from trips to the veterinarian with its mother and siblings, your new Poodle puppy may never have been in a car before. Now it not only has to get into this strange-smelling moving contraption, but also has to do so with some strangers!

It is always recommended that a traveling canine ride in a carrier for safety. The first ride home is no exception. *Never allow a dog—puppy or adult—to ride unrestrained in an automobile!*

Begin Training

It is important that you start training the very minute you get home. Before you take your Poodle inside to check out its new habitat, go immediately to the location you have cho-sen to be your pup's main "relief area." Let the puppy nose around and explore. (Some dog

experts recommend "salting" this area with urine-soaked litter and some feces from the pup's original home.) You want the Poodle to realize that this is the right place to urinate and defecate. This is the first step in house-breaking your Poodle. It is also one of the most important steps!

Wait patiently with your new dog. Don't pet or play with it. You want the puppy to start things off right by relieving itself at the appro-priate spot of *your* choosing. When the new-comer does this at the appointed place, praise and pet the young pup enthusiastically. This should be the reward the Poodle comes to expect and look forward to whenever it does what you want it to do. Establish that idea right at this spot, right now!

The right time to buy the equipment you will need for a new puppy is before it is needed, not after. These youngsters will soon outgrow this basket and will need adequate products to help with their feeding, training, and grooming.

Note: *Never, never* scold your Poodle at this important place! The relief spot is for relief followed by a reward. Don't ever confuse the Poodle by reprimanding it at this place.

Introducing the Pup to Its New Home

After your puppy's introduction to and reward at the relief spot you can take it inside to its new home. This is also a good time to introduce the cage/crate/carrier that will serve as the dog's special place inside your Poodle-proofed home. After giving the puppy a chance to look around and meet the other members of your family, put the probably tired animal in the crate, which should be located in an out-of-the-way—but not isolated—area.

You may have placed some familiar toys and perhaps a bit of old blanket from the dog's original home in the crate. Puppies get tired quickly. This need for a nap, combined with the comforting smells of its mother and siblings, will make the cage/crate/carrier seem less threatening. When you sense that your new canine family member is getting tired and needs a break, gently place it in the crate, shut

POODLE POINT

All the members of your household need to have a positive attitude about your Poodle's crate. The crate isn't a little prison—it is a special place in your home for your special pet.

the door, and walk away. Soon a bright young Poodle may break off contact with the others in the household when it needs a break and go, by itself, to the relaxation of its own little den.

You have another agenda for placing the tired youngster in its cage/crate/carrier. You want the puppy to associate the den with "tired," because this is where the pup is to rest and sleep. You must get this important lesson across to your new pet, for settling in is the next step in your Poodle's new life with you and your family.

Helping Your Poodle Adjust

Your Poodle puppy will now have to learn without the aid of its first teacher, its mother. You and your family will have to teach this pup what it needs to know to be happy and to make you happy within your home. This is an adjustment time for the puppy, but it is also an adjustment time for you and your family. It is important that each human in your household be consistent with the puppy. Fail in this and life will only be harder for this innocent youngster.

The pup must learn that when it is placed in its den at night, it should go to sleep. You and your family must learn to let this happen! A key commandment for you and each person that shares your home is that *nobody can give in to feeling sorry for the new crying, whining puppy out there in its crate.* If anybody slips out and takes the sad creature out of the crate to hug it and make it feel happy again, this person is guilty of doing real harm to the Poodle. The dog must come to realize that it can't cry each time it is lonesome, bored, or just wants to be petted and loved. Dog pounds are full of dogs that never learned this lesson!

Helping a Poodle adjust to a new home requires some time and patience. Without this adjustment time, some dogs may fail to ever truly settle in.

First-Night Blues

There are some ways to make the first few nights a bit easier for the pup. You can speak to the pup with a calm and reassuring voice, but don't overdo it. You want to let the puppy know that you are close by. You can place the "smells of Mom and home" things in the crate. You could also add an old-fashioned, nonleaking hot-water bottle to provide a semblance of its mother's warmth. You might put the water

Miniature and Toy Poodles don't know they aren't as big as the largest Standard Poodle. They need to be safeguarded in interactions with larger and more aggressive canines.

bottle in a canvas bag that will resist the sharp little teeth of a puppy. Don't use an electric heating pad, which might get chewed on, resulting in a fatal shock. Some people place

an old windup alarm clock with a loud ticking sound that seems to remind the pup of its mother's heartbeat. Still others turn on a radio very low near the crate. The radio is tuned to an all-night talk station, which seems to be helpful in putting the puppy to sleep.

The first few nights may be difficult. You and your family have already come to love this curly-haired little Poodle and want only to see it happy. It doesn't seem happy there, all alone in its crate. Steel your resolve not to change the situation and your puppy will soon adjust to the crate, its sleeping time, the absence of its mother, brothers, and sisters. If you falter now, this adjustment can take much longer and may not happen at all!

Starting Your Poodle Off Right

Your relationship with this bright young Poodle has just begun. You must remember the important part consistency plays in your becoming a good dog owner and your Poodle becoming a good pet. Properly conducted, the ownership of this Poodle pup can become an extremely gratifying experience. Handled improperly, you may wish that you had never wanted a dog.

Shaping this malleable young dog will take time, patience, understanding, and that old standby—consistency. If you add these elements to the base that you have in a good young Poodle, stir kindly and lovingly, following the recipe set forth by experienced Poodle people, you should be able to produce a quality pet. Because Poodles are fairly long-lived, you may have fifteen or more years with your dog; these early days will prove to be the most significant.

POODLE POINT

Changing diets for a new Poodle is always a mistake. Unless you have no choice, stick with the same food the dog or puppy has been eating and make any changes very gradually.

Whether a puppy or an older dog, the right Poodle will need a home that centers on the pet's comfort, safety, and care. These youngsters will not reach their Poodle-potential without just such homes.

Rehoming Older Poodles

While perhaps not needing all the special attention that puppies call for, adult Poodles brought into your home will still need time to adjust to a new setting, new rules, and new humans. Be patient and consistent in teaching the older Poodle (especially if this is a rescued dog) the lessons needed to be a new pet. Most Poodles are quite bright and will readily catch on to what is required. Be sure to show a good deal of love, attention, and consistency in the first weeks after bringing a new adult Poodle into your home.

This beautiful white Poodle represents generations of careful dog breeding, grooming advances, and excellent canine care.

"Poodle-proofing" your home should ensure a safe environment for your dog. Most Poodles are house pets; therefore, Poodle-proofing should take comfort and safety to a logical extreme. There are two phases of Poodle-proofing.

The First Phase

Begin with a critical look at your entire home, especially in those places where your puppy will live or to which it will most likely have even occasional access. Look for potentially dangerous places like:

1. Stairwells, landings, and balconies from which a young puppy might jump or fall.

2. Narrow spaces behind large appliances or heavy furniture where a pup could go and become trapped.

3. Low-level vents in laundry rooms or bathrooms that could catch an inquisitive youngster's head or that might have sharp edges that could injure a puppy.

4. Low cabinets that might entice a puppy when you aren't watching. Things we sometimes keep in floor-level cabinets (cleaners, pesticides, heavy pots and pans) can kill or injure little dogs.

5. Open fireplaces where a youngster could come in contact with stacked logs that could fall on it or artificial logs that could contain toxic materials.

6. Anything that is precariously balanced, such as heavy books or a radio on a bedside table.

The Second Phase

This involves searching for all those small items, perhaps long unnoticed, that could hurt or kill an inquisitive, innocent puppy, which learns by sniffing, licking, and chewing things. Some things to look for are:

1. Thumbtacks, nails, pins, needles, pennies (especially toxic because of the zinc content), and other tiny things that could be swallowed.

2. Lead-based paint on furniture, doors, walls, or baseboards.

3. Pesticides, cleaners, toiletries, air fresheners, mothballs, and household chemicals.

4. Furniture, rugs, draperies, and other household items that have been cleaned with chemicals that could be irritating, or even toxic, to a puppy or older Poodle.

Puppy-proofing your home begins with getting down to a pup's level and perspective to spot dangers you might otherwise miss.

YOUR HOME

Most homes are filled with poisons and other toxic chemicals that can kill an inquisitive Poodle puppy. Note that baker's chocolate and antifreeze are among them. Dogs love both of them, but they can mean death.

There are many small items that can be swallowed by a puppy. True puppy-proofing will remove these things from areas to which the dog has access.

5. Electrical wires, appliance cords, electrical outlets, entertainment centers, computer connections, and telephone connections.

6. Sharp edges, narrow slits where a pup's head could get caught.

7. Potentially poisonous houseplants.

8. Outside things like quick, easy access to busy streets, driveways, carports, or garages; de-icers, antifreeze (dogs love the taste of antifreeze and it can be deadly to them), poisonous yard plants, fertilizers, and weed killers.

Poodle-proofing must be done carefully. It should also be done with an eye to the future growth of your Poodle. Actually get down on the floor, like a puppy, and look carefully for things that could harm your new houseguest.

When you share your home with a pet, especially a pet like a bright, inquisitive Poodle, you must be extra sure that nothing within your home or the Poodle's environment can do harm. An untended chocolate bar within reach of a Poodle puppy, a leftover battery, or a long-lost pill can mean a very sick youngster.

Poodles deserve a safe environment and the Poodle owner is the only one who can make sure that this happens. Poodle-proofing isn't a one-time event, it is a continuous responsibility that can have a direct impact on the health of your pet. Don't neglect this very important aspect of pet ownership. Encourage the other members of your household to always keep potentially harmful or deadly things out of the reach of your Poodle.

FEEDING YOUR POODLE

Feeding a balanced and consistent diet rivals training and medical care in overall importance to the well-being of your Poodle. Many strides have been made in the field of canine nutrition, but one element remains constant—the human factor. Knowing what your Poodle needs to eat and why should be combined with a strong desire to feed the right food in the right way.

Balance Is Everything

What you feed your Poodle is going to have a direct and ongoing impact on the physical and mental health of the animal. It may also affect the dog's longevity, stamina, and personality.

Most importantly, your Poodle will need a balanced diet. This means a diet that is nutritionally complete and contains all the elements your dog will need to grow and to build strong bones, teeth, muscles, and that thick and curly coat.

There are five important rules to follow in feeding your Poodle:

1. Find a high-quality, nutritionally balanced dog food and stick with it consistently.

A balanced diet will help your Poodle build strong bones and muscles and a beautiful thick coat.

2. Keep plenty of clean, fresh water readily available. Water is important to your Poodle's daily nutritional program.

3. Don't overfeed your Poodle with either its usual food or treats.

4. *Never* feed table scraps!

5. If you have to change foods, do so very gradually.

6. It is very easy to overdo vitamin/mineral supplements. Use these products only after consultation with your Poodle's veterinarian.

Special Poodle Feeding Considerations

Dogs of all breeds with long or thick coats need more special nutrition to keep these coats in good shape than do most short-haired dogs. Discuss with your breeder what the Poodle was

This young Poodle will need a high-quality diet throughout his entire life. He will need to start with a great puppy food, then move on to equally great adult food, and then settle on a diet for older dogs. The accent is on quality and owner consistency at each age.

nents: proteins, carbohydrates, fats, vitamins, minerals, good drinking water, and its owner's adequate knowledge and consistency.

Proteins

The proteins in your Poodle's diet provide the amino acids necessary for growth; development of strong bones and proper musculature; ongoing maintenance of the bones and muscles; and the repair of injuries to the latter. Proteins also help combat sickness and aid in the healing process, providing essential building blocks for the production of infection-fighting antibodies. Proteins are important in the ongoing production of the enzymes and hormones that keep chemical processes functioning inside your Poodle.

Some sources of protein in dog foods are: poultry, usually chicken; meat items like beef and lamb; milk products; and some grains. Other sources listed on your Poodle's food packaging also contribute to overall protein levels.

Carbohydrates

Along with fats, carbohydrates are another energy source that fuels your Poodle and keeps it on the go. Measured in calories, carbohydrates in your Poodle's diet are generally provided by cooked grains and other vegetable ingredients.

Fats

Fats, another fuel for your Poodle, are a much more concentrated energy source than

being fed to maintain its healthy coat before you acquired the dog. You might also ask several other Poodle breeders what they do. Talk with your veterinarian about what kind of diet your Poodle requires for its coat's health.

Building Blocks of Good Canine Nutrition

Good nutrition doesn't just happen. For your Poodle to have a truly balanced and healthful diet, its food must contain several key compo-

POODLE POINT

Nutritional balance is very important in feeding a Poodle. Bear in mind that table scraps provide no dietary balance at all.

The excellent coat on this apricot Standard bespeaks a diet rich in proteins and other ingredients that make such a coat possible. Whether your Poodle is a show dog or a family pet, it will need the best possible food.

carbohydrates. In fact, fats provide more than twice the energy quotient of what an equal amount of carbohydrates can. Fats are also important in transporting the key vitamins A, D, E, and K into your Poodle's metabolic system. These vitamins are crucial to, among other things, helping keep your dog's skin and thick coat healthy. Fats also help maintain a healthy canine nervous system.

As with many human foods, fats also make dog foods more palatable—that is, taste better. Palatability is very important in ensuring that

your pet will enjoy its regular food and eat it in the proper amounts.

Vitamins

One area of canine nutrition that leads to some confusion and misunderstanding is a food's vitamin level. Generally, a high-quality, balanced dog food will contain all the vitamins your Poodle will normally need. Sometimes a well-meaning but underinformed pet owner will administer vitamins that aren't really necessary. But unless your veterinarian suggests a specific

Just as with human children, Poodles need a balanced diet free from excessive sweets, scraps, and treats that will upset dietary balance.

prescription vitamin, most of the time there is no need to supplement a dog's diet this way.

Minerals

Minerals play key roles in a balanced diet. They are essential for your Poodle's normal body functioning. Calcium, phosphorus, and magne-

sium are necessary for developing and maintaining strong teeth, bones, and muscles. Sodium and potassium aid in regulating bodily fluids and in maintaining your Poodle's nervous system. Iron in your dog's diet provides the basis for hemoglobin formation and healthy blood.

As with vitamins, if you are feeding your Poodle a high-quality dog food that is nutritionally balanced, normally you shouldn't need to supplement its diet with minerals. Before you provide mineral supplements, talk to your veterinarian or to a canine nutritionist.

Water

There is no more important ingredient in a balanced diet than clean, fresh drinking water. Your Poodle will need a ready source of water every day, provided in clean water bowls that are kept full and in easy access. Water bowls should be washed regularly with soap and warm water and thoroughly rinsed before you refill them. You wouldn't want to drink warm, smelly water out of a slimy, dirty, algae-laden receptacle; neither does your Poodle!

Knowledge and Consistency

All the other building blocks for good nutrition and a balanced diet (protein, carbohydrates, fats, vitamins and minerals, and water) won't do your Poodle much good without the final element: your knowledge and your consistency in feeding your pet.

Your Poodle is in a closed environmental system. It must be totally dependent on you for

Dogs need lots of clean, fresh water to keep them in good condition. Never let water bowls get slimy, algae-ridden, or foul-smelling.

POODLE POINT

Vitamins and minerals should come from a quality pet food. Use diet supplements with great care and only after consulting your veterinarian.

its food. Take time to thoroughly understand just what a balanced diet is. You will want to know how to gauge the quality of a food from its label. You need to know how to feed your Poodle at the different stages of its life.

Treats

Treats, and especially nutritionally balanced treats, can be tasty little tidbits for your pet. Unfortunately, like vitamins and minerals, treats can easily be overdone. This is especially true with charming Poodles that live in such close

The quality of your Poodle's health, coat, conditioning, and general activity level will be determined in large part by the quality of the dog foods you feed it.

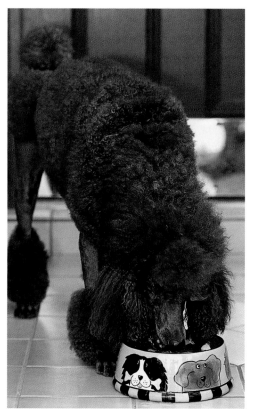

A Poodle owner can expect no more out of a Poodle in the way of physical activity than what goes into that Poodle through the food dish. Good nutrition, next to health care and training, is extremely important in the life and health of the dog.

contact with their humans. Some Poodles are so spoiled with treats that they will not eat their regular dog food. This promotes a lack of the all-important balance in a dog's nutrition level.

Treats can also contribute to the great companion canine malady—obesity. Use treats sparingly and they will mean more to the dog.

Handle treats for your Poodle the same way we should all handle rich desserts for ourselves!

Age Considerations

Feeding requirements change as your Poodle grows from a young puppy, to an adult, to an older dog.

Young Poodles

Under One Year Old Poodle puppies have a lot of growing to do and need the best possible nutritional start in life. Mother's milk has given

Poodles engaged in rigorous athletic activities will need sufficient vitamins and minerals in their diets to withstand such physical involvement. Active dogs will need more in their diets than the more sedate house pet.

them a good beginning. It is up to you to continue what she started. As with any other diet, and even more so at this stage, balance is crucial for the healthy development of a Poodle puppy. Without a quality balanced diet no puppy can be expected to reach its genetic potential.

A good rule to follow: puppies need twice as much complete nutrition as mature dogs do. A key puppy-feeding rule: stay with whatever your pup was eating when you got it! Puppies need a lot of nourishment and you can keep food before them all the time.

Adult Poodles

Over One Year Old Physical maturity for the three sizes of Poodles occurs at somewhat different times, but on average adulthood is reached at about one year or a year and a half. With adult status come some new feeding requirements. The puppy food that started your Poodle off should gradually be changed to an adult dog food that will be more balanced for the needs of a grown rather than a growing dog.

If your adult Poodle is involved in retrieving, obedience trials, breeding, or vigorous exercise, it may need more fats and proteins in its diet than a less active Poodle will need. Poodles are usually active and sprightly dogs, but extra activities also need to be considered when planning the dog's diet.

If your male Poodle has been neutered or your female spayed (as all nonshow and nonbreeding Poodles should be!), you will want to guard against your pet's becoming too fat. This can be handled in several ways:

1. Feed the dog as if it were an older animal.

2. Be certain that your Poodle gets adequate exercise.

3. Cut back on the volume of what the dog eats and eliminate most treats and certainly *all* table scraps.

Your adult Poodle will still need regularity and consistency in its feeding. Don't constantly switch foods any more for an adult than you would for a puppy. Find a diet and feeding schedule that works for you and your Poodle and stick with it!

Older Poodles

Eight Years Old and Older Older canines experience metabolic changes that require subsequent dietetic changes. As a dog's system slows down, energy providers in the diet will become less crucial. Many senior dog foods contain less fats. There may also be a somewhat lower percentage of protein in some senior diets.

Obesity

Owner knowledge and consistency becomes more important in an older pet than in an adult. Correctly feeding an older Poodle is almost as important as correctly feeding a puppy! Far too often one will hear the owner of an older and

A Standard Poodle and a Miniature Poodle show the classy good looks of the breed, which make this one of the most popular breeds of all time.

overweight dog say something like, "My Poodle always eats a full bowl of his food twice a day and has since he was a puppy." That Poodle, at eight or nine, isn't a puppy anymore and food amounts need to mirror what the dog needs, *not* what dog wants as far as quantity is concerned.

Obesity is a real killer in dogs. It not only makes a dog's life more miserable, but also can shorten that dog's life! Canine obesity can lead to or worsen other health issues like diabetes, heart disease, and arthritis. An overweight Poodle is an unhealthy Poodle at any age.

TRAINING YOUR POODLE

Poodles are bright, easily trained dogs with much to offer an owner or a family. Good behavior not only makes the dog more pleasant to be around, but serves also to keep the Poodle safe inside and outside the home.

Every Poodle, no matter what its size—Toy, Miniature, or Standard—needs and deserves good training. In fact, a dog of any breed or any size without training is an incomplete pet.

Your Poodle and Pack Behavior

It may be hard to imagine the cute Toy, the energetic Miniature, or the stately Standard Poodle as being bound by the same laws of nature that control packs of wolves or wild dogs. Pack behavior is a powerful force in the lives of any canine, whether purebred or of mixed breed.

Well-behaved Poodles don't just happen; they are shaped by their owners through careful, patient, and consistent training.

Your Poodle's pack must include you, each member of your household, and any other pets you may have. Under usual circumstances your Poodle will already be conditioned for pack behavior. This happens in its brief, but crucial, stay with its mother and littermates. Lessons in appropriate pack behavior began for your pup even before its eyes opened. In fair but very clear ways, a mother dog can impress her baby with what things are right and wrong in its limited world. In doing this she sets the stage for your dog's training and behavior for the rest of its life.

The first thing for you to learn and understand about dog training is the key role pack behavior plays in the way a dog sees itself and others. You can greatly aid your Poodle by building on this natural form of regulated behavior training. You and your family must fill the pack role for your

Not every Poodle will be a circus performer, but the same training skills used to teach the intricate tricks and actions in the center ring are those used by the owners of pet Poodles to get good behavior. Like the circus dog, the pet dog will respond to the right kind of treatment.

Poodle, and *each human must be higher than the dog in the pack ranking!*

Using Pack Behavior to Make Training Easier

Your Poodle's mother has already initiated training. If you follow her model, you and your dog will have a much easier training time. The mother dog's early training followed this format:

• She always treated each littermate *fairly*. The mother dog didn't ignore bad behavior, but neither did she overreact to it.

• She punished a misbehavior *immediately*, while the pup's short attention span could connect the reprimand with the misdeed.
• She punished *without anger*. She didn't injure the puppy physically or continue to scold it with barks and growls to modify its behavior.
• She treated her puppies in a *consistent* manner. She didn't reward bad behavior one time and then punish her offspring for similar behavior the next time. The fledgling minds of the little Poodles soon identified Mom's displeasure with certain acts that shouldn't be repeated. The mother also didn't ostracize a pup because of some bad behavior, withholding love in an attempt to gain obedience.

Understanding Training Concepts

The most essential element to understand about training is consistency. Follow these training concepts correctly and consistently and your Poodle will usually be quite easy to teach.
✔ **Have a regular time for training each day:** Training times should be free from distractions. Keep your training times short (not more than 10 or 15 minutes). Keep these times dedicated to the work of training and not just extensions of playtime.
✔ **Remember that you are the pack leader:** Be centered on the training. Be consistent. Keep your voice firm and businesslike. This lets your pup know that training time is different from

This Poodle is excelling at agility, just one of several activities that are open to some dogs and their owners who wish to pursue them. Agility, like obedience, is built on the same basic training skills that all Poodles should learn.

family time, feeding time, playtime, relief walks, or any other activities.

✔ **Set clear and reasonable training goals:** Before you begin a training session, have definite and realistic expectations for that session. It is very easy for novice dog trainers to expect too much too soon. Handle training in small steps and you'll be surprised at how much you and your Poodle can accomplish.

✔ **Make each training session a class:** Even though your Poodle probably won't need the extended rote repetitions some breeds might require, each training time must be conducted as a class with a single goal.

✔ **Stay with one well-defined objective:** Poodles are usually very bright and able to learn most clearly taught lessons and so may actually get bored with constant repetition, especially with the things they already know.

✔ **Use praise effectively:** Even though you have bonded with, and have come to love, this eager young dog, during training sessions use praise as a reward.

✔ **Give immediate and appropriate correction:** As in the training model provided by your Poodle's mother, corrective guidance should be immediate, right on the spot. If you delay providing your dog with such immediate guidance about some misdeed or some mistake in obeying a command, you will find that you have lost the opportunity to amend the behavior.

Some people erroneously believe that small dogs, like this Toy Poodle, don't need as much training as do larger dogs. Nothing can be further from the truth. All dogs deserve the best possible training.

trainers. Poodles, perhaps due to their long centuries of association with human beings, are quite different from a number of other dog breeds in ease of training. Being able to structure what your pet learns and make certain that you both can recognize and undo any unwanted behaviors your Poodle may learn on its own is one key to successful Poodle ownership.

House Training

Begin house training (or housebreaking) with the knowledge that regardless of how much your Poodle puppy may want your approval, on average it will have limited bladder control until it is about six months old. That does not mean you have to wait until the middle of its first year to begin house-training lessons. It does mean, however, that you can expect some accidents, and that these are probably based on physical immaturity.

You can start house training your new Poodle the day you bring it home. Have a waste-elimination spot already chosen. The key is anticipating the youngster's need to go, taking the dog to the right spot, waiting until it urinates or defecates, and then enthusiastically praising the pup for doing what it needed to do at the place you designated.

Crate training (see page 62) can greatly assist your Poodle in not only becoming house trained, but also in becoming familiar with its new home in the safest manner possible.

✔ **Be patient:** Poodles are among the smartest creatures in the canine world. They are also affectionate and very anxious to please you. Even with these two positives, some Poodles, and some Poodle trainers, don't progress at the same speed.

✔ **Be smarter than your Poodle:** Most Poodles are very quick to learn, and this is sometimes a problem for novice dog owners or amateur dog

POODLE POINT

House training your adult Poodle or your Poodle puppy isn't that hard to do, especially if you are patient and consistent in your efforts.

POODLE POINT

Thorough training can open up many areas of fun for you and your Poodle. Obedience trials and retrieving are just two of the possibilities.

There are several key things that can aid in house training your Poodle:

✔ Recognize that puppies will usually need to go out after eating. Young dogs only have so much room inside. Feeding them will cause the need to evacuate waste. Drinking water will soon require a trip out to urinate. Additional pressure on the bladder or colon from eating or drinking naturally makes waste relieving a high priority for a puppy.

✔ Use the same relief spot (if possible) as the place for the puppy to go. An older dog can adjust to relieving itself while out on walks with you, but a puppy needs great sameness or consistency early in its life.

✔ Use praise as a reward in all aspects of training, including house training. Doing what gets praise will become almost instinctual to the dog.

✔ Feed a high-quality, highly digestible puppy food. The stools with this type of food (such foods are usually in a dry form) will be smaller and firmer. Smaller and firmer stools are less runny, easier for a puppy to "hold in," and easier to clean up if an accident does happen.

✔ *Never* feed table scraps. Not only are scraps nutritionally unbalanced, but they may bring on diarrhea and/or vomiting.

✔ Leave out a small amount of food for your Poodle puppy but gradually as the pup matures establish specific feeding times.

Even though two dogs may contentedly live in the same home, each must be trained individually. Trying to work with two young dogs at the same time makes training nearly impossible.

✔ Avoid putting food or edible treats in your puppy's crate. The puppy will want this refuge to be as clean as possible. Food items in a crate will only cause a mess.

✔ Don't let mistakes become repetitive by failing to adequately clean them up. Always thoroughly clean and deodorize accident spots, but never punish or humiliate a puppy if it makes a mistake.

The best possible place for most dogs to void their waste is outside at a pre-selected location. Most Poodles easily learn this type of house training if it is begun while they are very young puppies.

Paper Training

A less efficient and less effective way to housebreak your Poodle is to use newspapers instead of the outdoor relief spot. Papers, usually spread around in a laundry room or bathroom, are a poor substitute. When combined with crate training, the outside method is almost foolproof with the vast majority of Poodles.

Paper training may be the only option for some people, especially those who have to leave a puppy alone for some period of time during the day. Also, high-rise apartment buildings and other living arrangements make a rapid trip to an outdoor relief spot inconvenient if not impossible. Nonetheless, paper training is not nearly as effective in house training as having a relief spot outside.

Crate Training

Crate training, unknown just a few decades ago to a majority of pet owners, is an excellent way to help your Poodle become a really good housemate. The use of crate training works in housebreaking because of your puppy's natural instincts to keep its primary sleeping area as clean as possible.

Novices and people who don't own a dog sometimes initially have a negative view of crates and crate training. This view is due to their general lack of understanding of two key points of innate dog behavior:

1. Dogs are by nature denning creatures. Dens give them not only a place to sleep out of the elements, but a place of their own to go when pursued, sick, injured, or in whelp.

2. Canines in the wild do not want to draw predator attention to their den areas. Feces and urine odor is one certain way to give away a den's location, and must be avoided.

Puppies are taught by their mothers that making messes in the sleeping area is taboo.

The crate or den must always be viewed as a place of refuge for your pet, not a miniprison. Use of the crate not only in housebreaking, but also in general Poodle ownership, can be managed better with the following hints:

✔ Keep a positive attitude, and encourage your family to do the same, about your Poodle's crate.

✔ When selecting a crate, buy one based on the size that your Poodle will ultimately reach.

Crate training is an extension of a dog's natural denning instinct. While some dogs may sleep in beds and others on mats, both of these would be better served if they were placed in a crate or carrier.

Partitions can make the crate the most appropriate size for a growing puppy so you won't have to purchase a series of ever larger crates for this purpose.

✔ Place your Poodle's crate in an out-of-the-way, but certainly not isolated, location in your home. Keep the crate out of direct sunshine, direct drafts, or in other places where temperatures will fluctuate significantly.

✔ Place your young Poodle in its den when it needs to rest, and for those times when you will not be able to supply adequate supervision, or when your puppy will be in harm's way (during parties, when you are moving furniture, when you are shopping or are otherwise away for a few hours, during spring-cleaning time, and so forth).

✔ Always take the puppy *directly* outside when you let it out of the crate. When the pup performs its duties at the relief site, praise it enthusiastically.

✔ Don't make release from the crate a reward in and of itself. Don't praise or play with the puppy (except for praise at the relief site) for ten minutes or so after it gets out of its crate.

✔ Put a sleeping mat (preferably a machine-washable one) in the appropriately sized crate. A couple of toys also can make the den/crate more homey for a Poodle puppy.

✔ Do not put food or water in the crate. This will only make the crate messy, which your pup does *not* want. Keep food and water in a regular location *outside* the crate.

✔ If your young Poodle whines, cries, or barks in the crate, use a calm voice to quiet the pup (see "Helping Your Poodle Adjust," page 43, and "First-Night Blues," page 43).

✔ Continually reinforce the positives of the crate and of crate training to the other members of your household.

✔ When you are training your Poodle, give it a "cool-down" period in its crate right after the training session and before starting to play with the dog.

When to Begin Training

Your Poodle puppy may have surprised you already by its quickly becoming house trained, learning its name, and coming to you when you call. Because of their keen intelligence, many Poodles grasp these early lessons and fit into the household so well that further training seems a task that can wait. But don't be lulled into this kind of thinking. Now is a good time to start training on a more advanced level.

Training Equipment

Dog training requires some basic equipment. Poodle equipment needs will vary according to the size of your dog—Toy, Miniature, or Standard. Equipment you will need:

✔ A "choke" collar—misnamed because it shouldn't choke—that is used to restrain your dog and remind it about a behavioral issue. This collar is for training purposes *only*. It should be large enough to slip over your pup's head when you put it on but with only about an inch (2.5 cm)

The "sit" command uses gentle pressure to lift the dog's head while equally gentle pressure causes it to sit down. The verbal command "sit" is given at exactly the same time the other two parts of this lesson are done.

of clearance. Because some collars can damage the dog's coat, many Poodles don't wear any collar around the house. You will need a different collar (with proper identification and tags) for regular use on walks and trips away from home.

✔ With the training collar you will also need a training leash, or lead. This lead can be made of leather or nylon webbing and should measure 6 feet (about 2 m) long.

✔ Thoroughly familiarize your Poodle puppy with both the training collar and the training lead *before* you begin training.

The Five Basic Commands

Sit

The first basic command is *sit* and should be very simple to teach your Poodle, because the dog already knows how to sit down. Your role as the trainer is to teach this young Poodle to sit down when and where you want it to. One good, nonthreatening way to teach this command is to observe your Poodle, wait until it is about to sit, and then give the command *"Sit!"* followed by ample praise and a small tasty treat as a reward. Let this puppy know that it has done something good and that each time it does what you ask, the reward will be there.

> ## POODLE POINT
>
> One of the best approaches to training is teaching your pet to respond to a clicker. Clicker training is not only a good way to help a dog learn, but you can teach the pet that a click will mean praise and food treats for proper action and behavior.

The hand signal for the "stay" command resembles an upside-down version of the classic police signal for "stop." It is given while gently raising the dog's head and issuing the verbal command, "Stay."

Your bright young Poodle will soon get the idea, and sitting when the command is given will be part of the dog's routine.

Stay

The *stay* command is best taught after your Poodle has mastered *sit*. The *stay* actually starts with the pup in the sitting position. Don't try to go too quickly in teaching this next command. Even though your Poodle is bright, be certain that sitting on command is well-ingrained in its mind before you move on to the *stay*. The *stay* is important but sometimes a little difficult to teach, because your Poodle loves you and wants, quite naturally, to be with you.

As with the *sit* command, observe the sitting puppy. Keep the dog on your left side near your foot. Step away from the youngster and say *"Stay."* The young dog may not remain in the *sitting/stay* position very long. Be sure to

reward it for any length of *stay*, but if the puppy begins to move toward you, start over and redo the exercise. The *stay* command goes against everything the pup really wants, so be patient. Follow the command format consistently. Your Poodle will ultimately learn the *stay* command, though perhaps not as quickly as the *sit*, but as soon as it learns that staying is what you want, your dog will do so.

Heel

Once your Poodle puppy has thoroughly learned how to sit and stay, you can put some mobility into the dog's training by teaching it how to *heel*—that is, follow you closely. This command begins with your puppy in the sitting position on your left side, next to your left leg. By now you've probably developed a strong "alpha" voice, and should use it in conjunction with this command. The training lead, attached

The purpose of the "heel" command is to get your Poodle to walk with you, not ahead of you or behind you. The ultimate goal of the "heel" command is to advance to using no leash when practicing this command.

This is a well-trained corded Poodle in a **down** *position. Even an exotic Poodle like this one benefits greatly from basic training.*

position. Praise as reward must be given *only* when the puppy is doing what you want it to do—that is, walk next to your left foot.

This command must be carefully taught to a bright dog like your Poodle. If the puppy stops, don't just drag it all over the room or backyard. The object is not just to cover some ground, but to have your pet walk with you, stopping when you stop. The gentle pressure you exert through the lead should get the dog moving. Your praise, combined with minor corrections using the lead slap against your leg, should keep it moving.

Down

Down can be taught after the dog has learned the *sit* and the *stay*. The lead is used in a different manner this time to encourage the youngster to drop all the way down onto its belly and remain there. Instead of the upward pull in the *sit*, the *down* requires the lead to be

to the training collar, is held in your *right* hand, guided by your left hand. Using your dog's name instead of the sample one used here, say "Pierre, *heel.*" As you give this command, step out, leading off with your *left* foot. If your Poodle doesn't step out when you do, lightly pop the slack of the lead against the side of your leg to get the dog's attention. Continue walking. The pup should soon get the idea.

The lead will help keep the Poodle from scampering on ahead, trailing behind you, or shifting sides. You want the dog to *heel* by your *left* foot. Reward (especially praise in this instance) for heeling correctly is given on the move and ceases when the pup stops or leaves the correct

The "down" command is always done from a "sit" and "stay" position. The gentle downward pressure, the hand signal, and the verbal command "down" are done simultaneously.

Teaching the Poodle to come when you call should be done in an enthusiastic, cheerful manner. NEVER call the dog to you to scold or reprimand it for something. This can untrain the dog to obey this command!

gently pulled straight down, thereby causing the Poodle's head and chest to go downward also.

This can be best accomplished with toys and smaller Miniatures by simply taking the lead in your *right* hand and pulling it downward as you make a movement similar to the one made in the *stay* with the *left* hand. As if you were very slowly bouncing an imaginary basketball, turn your left palm downward and move it that way in front of the dog's face as you pull down on the lead with your *right* hand. Simultaneously, give the verbal command *"Down."* Reward for any length of *down.*

Come

This command, the *come*, may seem simple. Don't all dogs want to come to their owners? This may be true most of the time, but you want this very important command to work *all* the time. To effectively teach this command you will need the old standby, consistency, combined with lots of enthusiasm. You should always use your dog's name with this command, as in, "Pierre, *come*."

When beginning this lesson with a puppy, use your arms open wide and invite your loving pet to come to you. When it does come to you, give the dog a reward and lots of praise.

The *come* is one command that you can "unteach" faster than you can teach it. *Never* call your puppy to you for something unpleasant, like punishment or a scolding. Doing this can add doubt and hesitation in the dog's mind about

what the outcome of obeying this command will be. Just as no unpleasantness is allowed toward the puppy at the relief spot, no one in your household can be allowed to use the *come* to catch the dog for something the dog doesn't like. You don't want to teach your Poodle that *come* sometimes means something negative.

Obedience Classes

Your Poodle is very likely to excel in the basic commands. Always be patient in training a dog. Your dog may be slower to mature than others of the breed, of its strain, or even of its litter! Your training style may be inconsistent, or perhaps someone in your home has been undoing the training in a way you may not know about.

If you have any difficulty at all, or if you just want to meet a lot of dog owners who have the similar goal of a well-behaved companion pet, join a class on dog training. Your Poodle may be just the candidate for such a class and your training time can be significantly shortened.

Appearance is a major part of the Poodle. An ungroomed or poorly groomed Poodle fails to come up to the standard for looks that is one of the most defining aspects of the breed. A well groomed Poodle is more pleasant to be around and presents a better image for the dog and its owner.

For an indoor dog like the Poodle, with its dense and curly coat, good grooming is essential. Baths, brushing, teeth cleaning, and nail trimming can help make any pet a better companion. A dirty and smelly dog isn't very pleasant to be around. The smell can permeate an entire room, or an entire house.

Before You Start

Whether or not you believe you want to show your Poodle, you should learn about the various clips and general Poodle coat care. You could do this by talking with experienced Poodle breeders and exhibitors. You could also learn about Poodle coat matters from dog

Great grooming shows in this white Standard Poodle. Most Poodle owners can learn grooming or it can be done by professional groomers.

groomers. Unless you are really handy and grasp the grooming of your pet very quickly, start by using a professional.

Don't even contemplate being your own groomer (and most pet owners shouldn't) without taking time to learn what you are doing. Even to produce some of the simpler clips you will still need some training. Spare your Poodle your trial grooming efforts. Dog grooming, especially the clipping part, is an intricate and precise task. Learn about it before you undertake to do it yourself!

Professional Groomers

Nearly all owners of pet Poodles use dog groomers for some or all of their dog's grooming needs. (This is a strong recommendation for first-time Poodle owners!) Most owners of show Poodles do much or all of their own show grooming. Grooming for a dog show is an even

Many Poodle breeders and exhibitors do their own grooming. Many owners of pet Poodles use professional groomers, either exclusively or on an occasional basis.

more precise and painstaking activity than pro- fessionally grooming a household pet. A profes- sional dog groomer can make your new Poodle an attractive addition to your home and lifestyle. Groomers have all the facilities to wash, clip, trim, and otherwise provide for the overall appearance of your Poodle. Grooming charges vary from shop to shop, depending on where you live. If you factor in grooming charges when you make your decision to buy a Poodle, the costs can be budgeted and will not seem as expensive.

Grooming Tools

Many professional groomers and Poodle exhibitors have their individual ideas about how grooming should be done and what spe- cific tools you should use to do the grooming.

A general list of the *bare minimum* of grooming tools would include the following:

✔ A sturdy table with a skid-proof rubber mat on which to groom.

✔ A bathtub or sink large enough for your Poodle to be able to lie down on its side. This tub or sink should also have a skid-proof mat or surface to keep the dog from slipping or sliding around.

✔ Electric clippers of professional quality with several blades (#07, #10, and #15 are a good start).

✔ Straight scissors about 8 inches (20 cm) long.

✔ A fine-toothed and a coarse-toothed metal comb.

✔ A brush designed for Poodle grooming with nylon bristles or wire bristles set in rubber.

✔ A "slicker" brush with wire bristles bent at the ends.

✔ A hair dryer, preferably one designed for dog grooming.

✔ Towels, large and small.

✔ Special dog shampoo and a conditioner made for use on dogs.

✔ A spray or spritzer to give your Poodle's coat shine.

Bathing

Grooming starts with bathing your Poodle. Talk to experienced Poodle people and get some recommendations on what kinds of shampoos and conditioners they use, and why. You want to make certain that your shampoo fits the needs of the Poodle. Most shampoos for humans are not right for use on dogs.

One approach calls for you to wash the Poodle lying on its side in a tub filled only half full with moderately warm water. Keep the

This Poodle has been washed, rinsed, and is being dried. Groomers generally can handle all of these chores as well as clipping the Poodle as desired.

dog's head out of the water and soap and water out of the dog's eyes. Put cotton in your Poodle's ears to keep water out of them. Let the water get over, under, around, and through the coat on both sides of the Poodle.

Work up a lather, always remembering to protect the dog's eyes and ears. Don't miss any spots as you gently massage the shampoo into the curly coat. Wash first one side and then turn the dog over on its other side and do the same. Your efforts at getting the suds all the way to the dog's skin will require some elbow grease on your part.

Rinsing

As important as making sure that you thoroughly wash your Poodle may be, rinsing your dog is even more important. If you don't get all the shampoo out of the dog's coat, you can count on a bad-looking Poodle with skin irritations, a dull appearance, and a greasy feel. Rinsing should take you just as long as the bathing did. Rinse several times to make absolutely certain you get out all the shampoo. Thorough rinsing can be made much easier by a handheld shower nozzle.

Conditioners

Always know the proper way to use a conditioner. It is recommended that new Poodle groomers stick with products designed for dogs and not humans. With experience you may be able to use a conditioner designed for people, but stay with the products specifically for dogs until

you have more grooming experience. Working with a conditioner recommended by a groomer, an experienced Poodle exhibitor, or a skilled professional in a pet products store, use the product just as the directions say. Don't experiment on your dog; follow the instructions.

Drying

There are several approaches to drying a Poodle's curly coat. You should always start by using a thick towel to briskly dry the now washed, rinsed, and conditioned Poodle. Don't speed this job along. Be thorough and towel dry each part of your Poodle's anatomy.

After doing your best with a towel you could put your Poodle in its crate, which should, of course, be clean. Some Poodle groomers put the dog's crate on a sunny porch and let the animal dog dry naturally.

POODLE POINT

By starting early and continuing on a regular schedule, you can make grooming your Poodle no big deal for you, the groomer, or your dog.

This blue Standard shows off his style in a much shorter coat length than some of those seen in the show ring. Hunting retriever Poodles will have a similar clip to help them avoid briars and brambles and to move smoothly in the water.

Using an electric handheld hair dryer (unless you have access to one on a stand like the kind professional groomers use), choose a medium setting and take your time drying and brushing your Poodle. Dry one part thoroughly before moving to another location. Be careful not to burn your Poodle with the hair dryer by holding it too close to the dog or concentrating on one area too long at one time. Make certain that the Poodle is completely dry and you will have

a lot of fullness in the coat that you can now groom into any of several clips.

Poodle Clips

Learn the good points about each of the Poodle clips so you can decide which will be best for your Poodle.

The Puppy Clip

The puppy clip can be worn in dog shows by Poodles under one year old. This clip leaves the puppy's coat long, but the face, throat, feet, and base of the tail are shaved. There is a pompon at the end of the puppy's tail. This trim presents a smooth appearance and gives the

The three most popular Poodle clips in the United States: Top—The puppy clip; center—The English saddle clip; bottom—The continental clip.

These Standard Poodles have been clipped in a close and informal style much like the sporting clip. Such a clip shows off the physique of the dogs in a way that is easy for a dog owner to maintain.

puppy a refined, consistent, and unbroken line. Minor coat flaws can be scissored into a more pleasing shape.

The English Saddle Clip

The English saddle is one of two show clips for adult Poodles. It is considered one of the most intricate clips. Grooming methods are often used to help hide or de-emphasize some flaw or appearance shortcoming that a show dog may have. The English saddle clip can do sometimes do just that.

The English saddle calls for the face, throat, feet, forelegs, and base of tail to be shaved. Puffs are left on the front legs and the tail has a pompon. The hindquarters are left with a short blanket of hair with a curved area shaved out of each flank. The hind legs have two shaved bands.

Most of the main coat is left full and may be shaped for a balanced appearance. The entire foot is shaved and a shaven area shows above each puff.

The Continental Clip

The other adult show clip in the United States is the continental clip. The continental calls for the face, throat, feet, and base of the tail to be

An excellent grooming job shows off the profile of this apricot Poodle. This style is usually called the continental clip.

shaved. The hindquarters may either be shaved bare or have a ball-like pompon covering each hip. All four legs are shaved, with bracelets on the back legs and puffs on the front legs. The tail also has a pompon. The foot is similar to that in the English saddle, and so is the permitted trimming to complete a balanced look.

The continental is most often seen in American dog shows. It is similar to the "lion clip" often associated with the general public's perception of the Poodle, especially when the pompons on the hips are forgone in favor of the fully shaven hindquarters. You can learn much about the continental clip by visiting dog shows and watching exhibitors prepare their adult Poodles for the show ring.

The Sporting Clip

The most utilitarian of all the show Poodle clips, the sporting clip is allowed only in American Kennel Club dog shows in the special classes for stud dogs and for brood bitches. The sporting clip is also allowed in the parade of champions, in which past conformation champions, now

kept primarily as breeders or pets, are brought back for Poodle specialty shows. As with the other clips, the face, feet, throat, and base of the tail are shaved. The rest of the Poodle's coat is clipped or cut with scissors to about one inch (2.5 cm) in length and conforming to the dog's body outline. A scissored cap is left on the dog's head and the tail has the obligatory pompon.

The entire visual impact of the sporting clip is very pleasing. You can easily see the outline of the dog. The coat has a short, curly look. It is much easier to keep than other adult clips but maintains much of that elegant Poodle appearance.

The Retriever Clip

A clip that is very much like the sporting clip but that is allowed in AKC dog shows is the retriever clip. In the retriever clip the pompon and the scissored cap are gone and the Poodle's hair is cut much shorter than even in the sporting clip. The retriever clip gives the Poodle a real utilitarian look. Most of the work is done with clippers (using a #04 blade). This is a good look for your standard Poodle if you only want the dog as a companion. The ease of care and convenience of this clip make it popular with owners of dogs that aren't slated for the show ring.

It is important to remember that shaving, scissoring, and clipping all require some skill, experience, and manual dexterity. Unless you are careful, you could scrape, cut, or clipper burn your Poodle. No apologies are necessary

This white Standard Poodle is retrieving in the original continental clip. The extra hair was originally left to ward off the effects of cold water. The water and hair do not seem to be bothering this Poodle at all.

Playful and yet well groomed, this white Miniature seems to know that she looks good. Her appearance says volumes about her attitude and disposition.

for encouraging you to serve an apprenticeship with someone who really knows how to accomplish the visual miracles that occur when a good Poodle is correctly groomed.

An Overview

Start early Your Poodle will need to be carefully and consistently groomed throughout its entire life. Start a puppy early to get it accustomed to the sounds and feels of grooming. Gradually introduce your youngster to the whirring monster that humans recognize as a clipper. Don't frighten your Poodle with the clipper or you may always have a real chore when grooming time comes around.

Grooming, especially the regular brushing that is sufficient for most pet Poodles, can be a positive experience for you and the dog. For a young Poodle, a thorough combing and brushing is usually sufficient. Don't leave any matted or tangled places, or the next time you brush your Poodle will likely be a difficult session for you, and a painful one for your dog.

Brush your Poodle puppy's hair in the opposite direction from the way it grows. Do this without tugging or hard pulling. Soon, with continued brushing, the coat will be smooth and flexible and will easily yield to the brush. Finish this session with a thorough combing with a coarse comb and then follow up with a fine comb.

An adult Poodle is first brushed the way the coat is growing and then against the way the coat grows. Follow with a thorough coarse combing, completed by a thorough fine combing. Start at the Poodle's head and go down its neck onto its back, and then onto its tail. You then brush and comb down each side to the legs. Go on to the head and the ears, leaving the tail for last.

Because the Poodle coat needs regular attention to look its best, set a regular time for bathing, drying, brushing, and the other facets of nail trimming, teeth cleaning, and ear checking that will complete your Poodle's grooming routine.

MEDICAL CARE

Assuming the responsibilities of Poodle ownership must include consistent and timely medical care. Not only does this medical care have curative and aftercare aspects, but also the crucial element of prevention of illnesses and injuries.

Keeping Your Poodle in Good Health

Common sense is the centerpiece of any plan to keep your Poodle healthy, but can be enhanced by several recommendations:
✔ Avoid locations, situations, and conditions where there is a danger of potential injury or infection.
✔ Follow a careful regimen of a nutritionally balanced diet, lots of clean, fresh water, and regular exercise on a daily basis.
✔ Be parasite-conscious and keep your Poodle as free as possible from these health-robbing pests.

These Poodles clearly show their health and vigor. Such health and vigor comes from a responsible owner using a skillful veterinarian.

✔ Maintain a safety-first attitude by assuming that the worst can indeed happen; always use a leash outside fenced areas and *NEVER* leave your dog in a parked car, even on a moderately warm day.
✔ Establish and maintain a regular schedule of visits to your Poodle's veterinarian for checkups and ongoing preventive health care.

The Health Team Concept

You and your family will most obviously be key members of your Poodle's health team. As primary members who are around the dog everyday, you will be responsible for maintaining a safe environment, providing the right foods, and seeing to appropriate exercise. You also must arrange regular medical visits.

Your veterinarian will be the next member of this team. A veterinarian will help your new Poodle get off to a good start, nurture it

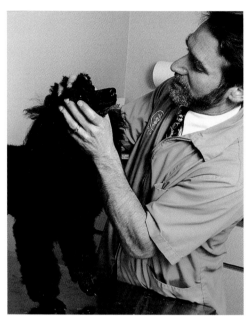

A knowledgeable veterinarian is a key component in the your Poodle's health team. Combined with the dog's groomer and your own watchful care, your Poodle should stay in good health.

Essential to any Poodle health team is a reliable dog groomer. Each time your Poodle is groomed, an alert, professional groomer can give you valuable information about small but important aspects of your dog's development and overall health. Groomers can spot skin conditions, hair quality, small injuries, parasites, and myriad such things that other team members may overlook.

Preventive Care

Regular visits to the veterinarian will provide an early warning of impending or potential health concerns. These scheduled checkups will also alert you to existing conditions that should be treated. Your veterinarian will keep your Poodle current on its immunizations, which are often required by law, as well as by your desire to have the healthiest dog possible. Where you buy your Poodle puppy can often be the single greatest factor in how many health concerns you will have to face in the life of your pet. Getting a Poodle from sound, healthy stock that is as free as possible from inherited conditions and defects won't guarantee an illness-proof pet, but it can greatly increase your chances of getting one!

through the days of its adulthood, and provide care in its senior years. A key to the best use of this important resource is to visit the veterinarian *before* problems arise, not just in medical emergencies.

Another significant member of your dog's health team should be an experienced Poodle person whose understanding of the breed will be an invaluable asset. This knowledgeable friend can add perspective to your Poodle's health needs by seeing the dog often enough to know it, yet infrequently enough to spot subtle changes that you might miss in your day-to-day contact with your pet.

Combine wise choosing of a Poodle with regular veterinary visits, a quality and balanced diet, and consistent care. Add to this prevention prescription a proactive attitude about avoiding pos-

POODLE POINT

Preventing health problems is smarter and less expensive than having to deal with health problems after they occur. It is also a lot better for the well-being of your Poodle.

sible disease and injury and your Poodle will have a much better chance of being the pet you want, because you have become the owner it needs.

Immunizations

Your Poodle's veterinarian can greatly help you understand what vaccinations your pet will need as a puppy and as an adult. The frequency of such vaccinations and the diseases for which they are administered are now quite different than they were just a few years ago.

The immunizations your Poodle will need are broadly grouped into three main categories: core, noncore, and not recommended. This information is crucial because Poodles are one of the dog breeds that are sometimes adversely affected by vaccinations. It is important that your veterinarian recognize that Poodles can be overvaccinated. Also, the "booster shots" that were once given annually are no longer recommended in many cases, because the vaccines for several infectious diseases (parvovirus, distemper, and hepatitis) can remain effective for seven years. The vaccination for rabies is the only one required by law (which differs from state to state); it can last up to three years.

Essentially, in some Poodles autoimmune diseases have actually been brought on by vaccinations. These diseases weaken the dog's system by responding negatively to its own tissue. You and your veterinarian should be fully aware of which vaccinations are core (essential), noncore (not always needed), or not recommended.

Fleas can be infested with a parasite themselves—the tapeworm that is passed on to your Poodle when it swallows a flea. Another reason for making your dog and environment flea free!

External Parasites

Fleas: The curse of many dogs' lives, fleas are the most common parasite affecting dogs. Like little vampires, fleas feed on your dog's blood and can cause anemia if the infestation is severe enough. Fleas are also hosts for another parasite, this one an internal pest: the tapeworm.

Occasionally a dog will develop a quite severe allergic reaction to fleas. Flea-bite allergy can make your Poodle absolutely miserable, causing severe scratching, hair loss, and much discomfort. Flea-bite allergy requires immediate veterinary diagnosis and care. The second phase of

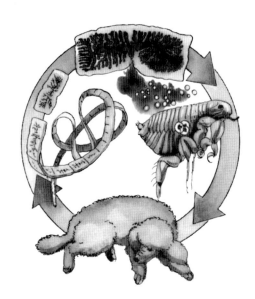

Full of life and fun, this Poodle provides ample evidence that she is healthy and happy. A healthy Poodle is a happy Poodle.

this confrontation means you have to banish fleas from your pet's life and lifestyle.

Show fleas no mercy. You must understand that fleas are among the worst parasitic enemies your dog has. The dog has no way to rid itself of these serious pests and must depend on you. Eradicating fleas from your Poodle's environment means going to all-out war against them. If your dog has fleas, everywhere your dog goes can have fleas. This will include your house, your yard, your car, your dog's kennel—anywhere the dog can get to. You must de-flea all of these areas, because if you miss even one you have failed: the fleas will have left eggs and pupae in that one remaining spot and can start up again from there.

Talk with your veterinarian and with other animal care specialists about the right weapons to use against the flea. Dips, shampoos, flea collars, dusts, and sprays are for use on the dog. Foggers, house sprays, carpet dusts and cleaners, and traps are all for use in your home or car.

Kennel sprays and yard treatments are designed for outdoor areas like your backyard. Also remember to treat any occasional places your dog may visit, such as your cottage at the lake.

Fleas spend 90 percent of their life cycle off the dog. It is the adult fleas, which make up about one-tenth of the total fleas in an area of infestation, that will actually be on your Poodle. Treating only the small portion on the dog and leaving the others to hatch, mature, and reproduce is a waste of time.

Ticks: Ticks are much larger bloodsuckers than fleas, but getting rid of them isn't quite as difficult. Many of the treatments and deterrents used for fleas will also work for ticks. For dogs, such as Poodles, that may be groomed with some of their skin showing, ticks can be an additional problem. Tick bites, and the incorrect removal of ticks, can cause infections and unsightly scarring that can detract from a Poodle's appearance.

Ticks can also bite you, so be very careful (perhaps using rubber gloves) when you remove a tick. They sometimes carry serious, life-threatening diseases, such as Rocky Mountain Spotted Fever and Lyme Disease. Ticks require diligence on the part of a Poodle's owner, but they don't usually involve the same widespread, lingering infestations that fleas do. It is a good idea to regularly inspect your Poodle after you have been places where ticks may be. The tight Poodle coat can help keep ticks from getting through to the skin, but it can also hide the ones that do get to the skin. Check the entire dog carefully, especially in tick-favorite locations like the ears, face, and neck.

Ear mites: Poodles can be susceptible to ear mites, another external pest that can make life miserable for your dog. These tiny pests inhabit the ear and the ear canal. A dark, dirty, waxy residue in the ears can signal an ear mite infestation. You can also tell that these microscopic bothers are around by observing your Poodle. If your dog vigorously shakes its head from side to side, or if it constantly paws at its ears, ear mites are a good possibility. Follow your veterinarian's recommendations as to treatment and eradication of these parasites. When you perform your regular checks of your Poodle's ears, always look for signs of ear mite presence.

Mange: There are two kinds of mange; both are caused by mites:

1. *Demodectic mange,* once called "red" mange, is a special problem with very young and very old dogs. Demodectic mange can cause very rough and patchy areas around the head, face, and eyes and in other places on an afflicted animal's body. Sometimes this version of mange can cause widespread hair loss and severe, painful itching.

2. *Sarcoptic mange* owes its presence to another mite that burrows into your dog's skin. It often causes severe hair loss and itching that can induce a dog to scratch itself raw. Sarcoptic mange has another side effect: it can also be transmitted to and from humans. On people it is usually short-lived, but it can cause itching and a rash.

There are dozens of suggested "home remedies" for both kinds of mange, but you will always be far wiser to consult your veterinarian. Follow this professional's advice both in treatment and in prevention of these ugly, uncomfortable, parasitic conditions.

Just because your Poodle is predominantly a house dog, don't become complacent about external parasites. Rats, mice, and squirrels can bring these problems right into your backyard or onto your deck, balcony, or patio. Walks in the park, a country outing, or even a relief trip outside could expose your Poodle to these pests whose lives depend on parasitically living off your pet.

Internal Parasites

These consist of various types of worms. Your veterinarian (despite the fact that many home-worming remedies are available) should be the first line of defense against these health robbers. Along with whipworms, your Poodle should be treated for the following.

Roundworms: Roundworms attack the health and vitality of dogs of any age. Puppies are especially vulnerable to them and may have had them introduced into their bodies even before the puppies were whelped. If a mother dog has roundworms she can pass them on to her litter.

Roundworms drain away the strength, vigor, and even physical potential of baby Poodles. Youngsters with roundworms will simply not grow and flourish with these internal pests. It is difficult enough for pups to gain the health and nutrition they need to reach their promise as mature dogs without having to share their health with a group of parasitic interlopers.

Maintaining a clean environment will greatly aid you in keeping roundworms and other pests away from your Poodle. Always quickly and appropriately dispose of stools. Use appropriate

POODLE POINT

Poodles can be bothered by a number of internal and external parasites. Regular visits to your veterinarian can help keep these health-robbers away from your Poodle.

sanitary measures to keep worms from getting a start with your dog. It is also good to remember that children and other humans can become infested with roundworms.

Hookworms: Like roundworms, hookworms can affect dogs at any time of their lives. Puppies, struggling to grow, are again especially vulnerable to hookworms. Hookworms attach themselves like tiny lamprey eels to the inside of a youngster's small intestine. These parasites thrive on the blood they siphon off the host animal. In so doing, hookworms greatly weaken the pup's ability to withstand disease and infection.

Clinical signs of hookworms are bloody or tarlike stools. Your veterinarian can finish off the hookworms before they do something that

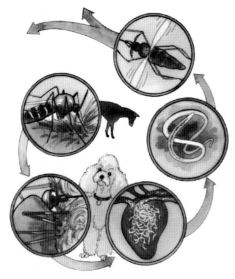

Mosquitos pass on heartworm larva from other animals already infected with heartworms. Untreated, these larva grow and can nearly clog a dog's heart, causing a lot of suffering and eventual death.

could lead to more serious health problems for your Poodle. Consult your veterinarian and then follow what this professional animal health person recommends.

Tapeworms: Fleas introduce tapeworm larvae into a dog's system. A tapeworm-infested Poodle will not become the family pet that it could be. Tapeworms, like other parasites, will take away part of a dog's physical reserves.

As with other parasites, the clearest course of action involves your veterinarian. Let the veterinarian advise you on overcoming both tapeworms and their delivery system, the flea.

Heartworms: Like the tapeworm, the heartworm is an unwelcome gift from an unwelcome pest: mosquitoes. Instead of the flea serving as host for the parasite, infected mosquitoes can introduce the heartworm into your Poodle. Heartworms were once a regional problem, but today much of the United States is on alert for these potential killers.

The heartworm gets into your pet's bloodstream through the bite of a mosquito that is a carrier for this parasite. Once inside your Poodle, heartworm larvae travel to the heart. Unless they are stopped by medication or other treatment, the heartworms will literally clog up a dog's heart. Death is almost always certain in untreated animals.

Veterinary medicine has produced a preventive that must be given on a regular basis. This will keep heartworms away from your pet's heart and ultimately prolong its life. If heartworms are not prevented in young adult animals, an expensive and perhaps dangerous treatment is possible. With heartworms, the prevention is much simpler than the treatment. Treatment is much kinder than letting a heartworm-infested pet die needlessly.

Good healthcare and a watchful owner will add years to this Poodle's life. Combined with good training, a quality diet and consistent medical care will make a big difference in this Poodle's life and lifestyle.

Other Medical Problems

Poodles, like dogs of all breeds, are targets for other health problems. Because a Poodle usually spends a lot of time in close contact with its human family, some of these health problems will be easier to observe.

Anal Gland Impaction

The anal glands are on either side inside the dog's anus. In the normal stretching and con-tracting during bowel movements, these glands are usually emptied of the foul-smelling secre-tions that collect there. If these glands become clogged or impacted, they cause a dog a great deal of discomfort and may have to be emptied by hand.

If you see your Poodle dragging its rear end along the floor in a "scooting" motion, impacted anal glands are a possible reason. Your veterinarian can easily teach you how to empty these glands or will do it for you. Don't let this common condition cause your pet unnecessary discomfort; pay attention to the anal glands!

Diarrhea

Most dogs will suffer from diarrhea at some times in their lives. Stress, rapid dietary changes, or internal parasites can be common causes of diarrhea. Although this condition is not usually serious, diarrhea can be a clinical signal of the beginnings of some serious ailment. Any diarrhea that continues for more than 12 to 24 hours, or that has traces of blood in the resultant stools, merits a visit to the veterinarian.

Vomiting

Vomiting, like diarrhea, is a fairly common canine occurrence. In puppies, too much excite-ment after eating can bring it on. Stress and changes in diet are also usual causes of ordi-nary vomiting. As with diarrhea, vomiting may be a sign of some more serious illness or condi-tion. Combined with diarrhea, vomiting can rapidly put a pup in serious shape from dehy-dration. Vomiting that lasts longer than 12 hours deserves a trip to the veterinarian.

Bloat

Bloat, or gastric torsion, is one of the most serious conditions for dogs. Usually affecting deep-chested dogs, which include standard Poodles (rarely Toys or Miniatures), bloat plagues enough Poodles to encourage all Poodle owners to play it safe and know about bloat. Bloat can destroy the life of an otherwise healthy and happy Poodle in just a few hours. It involves a swelling and twisting of a dog's stomach from water, gas, or a combination of the two.

Bloat and its causes are still something of a medical mystery. There is a list of what might cause a dog to bloat; some of these suggested reasons can evidently bring about bloat independently or can work in conjunction with other reasons. Some suggested causes are the following.
• A genetic predisposition in some breeds and in some families (or strains) within these breeds.
• Intense stress from any number of sources.
• Strenuous exercise following a large meal (particularly of dry dog food) and the intake of a large amount of water.
• The age of the dog. Dogs over 24 months of age seem to be more likely to bloat than younger animals.
• The sex of the dog. Males seem more susceptible to bloat than females.

Whatever the reasons or causes for bloat, gastric torsion is a real killer of dogs in the deep-chested breeds. Although your Poodle will probably not be as high on a list of bloat candidates as a Bloodhound or Great Dane, don't take chances on this dreaded condition.

Some clinical signs of bloat:
• Obvious abdominal pain and noticeable swelling in the abdominal area.
• Excessive salivation and rapid breathing.
• Pale and cool-to-the-touch gums and skin in the mouth.
• A shocked or dazed appearance.
• Repeated tries at vomiting with no vomitus coming up.

To have any chance at saving the life of a dog with gastric torsion, you must act immediately. Call your veterinarian and alert him/her of the possibility of bloat. Safely, but with all urgency, transport your Poodle to the animal clinic.

Special Health Concerns for Poodles

Some of the special health conditions afflicting Poodles are rare, others are more common, and many have a genetic or inheritable beginning. If you know of, or suspect, any of these disorders or abnormalities in your Poodle's background, discuss them with Poodle experts and consult a veterinarian for a complete checkup and recommended treatment methods.

Addison's Disease: This deficiency in adrenocortical hormones shows the common clinical signals of diarrhea, vomiting, overall lack of strength, and a general lack of good physical condition.

Epilepsy: The same neurological disorder that afflicts some humans, epilepsy can be recognized by seizures or convulsions when irregular electrical discharges to the brain are received. Epilepsy can be controlled through medication.

Hypothyroidism: This disorder stems from low hormone production levels in the thyroid. Clinical signs include irregular heartbeats, skin and coat problems, obesity, a lack of mental acuity, and a lack of energy. Hypothyroidism can be treated with prescription medicines.

Legg–Calvé–Perthes disease: This condition is caused by the deterioration of the upper parts of the femur, which can result in lameness in some Toy Poodles. This can be a fairly painful condition, but some dogs get over it and others require surgery.

Patellar luxation: This is a weakness of the kneecap in Toy Poodles; it can be repaired surgically. The kneecap slips out of position and causes some temporary lameness in the leg.

Progressive retinal atrophy (PRA): In this eye illness, the light cells of the retina don't receive enough blood. As a result these cells gradually deteriorate, causing blindness. This is a serious problem affecting some families of Poodles, Irish Setters, and other breeds. Because PRA can be identified by a veterinarian specially trained in diseases of the eye, the American College of Veterinary Ophthalmologists, through the Canine Eye Registration Foundation, has developed a registry and certification process to insure that Poodles, and dogs of other breeds, are annually certified as being clear of PRA and other inheritable eye diseases.

Poodles need nearness to their humans to become complete. Without human interaction, Poodles become miserable and often get into trouble.

Sebaceous adenitis (SA): Hair loss, a type of dandrufflike flaky skin, and smelly skin infections are all clinical signals of sebaceous adenitis. This chronic skin condition is brought about by irritated, often abnormal sebaceous glands. Antibiotics and regular bathing in special medicinal solutions may bring this disorder under control, but SA is also thought to be inheritable. Poodles with this ailment should not be allowed to reproduce and pass this condition on to successive generations. (The PCA has established a special fund to support SA research, especially in Standard Poodles.)

Von Willebrand's disease: This inherited, hemophilialike blood disorder stems from an abnormality in the dog's blood. Free bleeding is a key clinical symptom.

Canine hip dysplasia (CHD): This is a medical condition in which the hip joint is slack or loose. This slackness or looseness is combined with a deformity of the socket of the hip and the ball-like femoral head joining the thighbone. This malformation of the development of the hip and the connective tissues results in an unstable hip joint with an unsteady, wobbly gait that is clearly painful to the dog.

Although Poodles are not the highest in numbers of dogs with CHD, and then only in Standard Poodles, and although CHD is not clearly always caused by inherited genes, a wise Poodle purchaser would do well to be certain that the

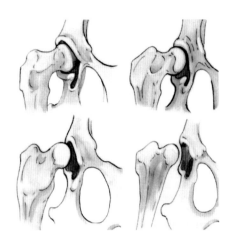

A visual explanation of hip dysplasia: Top left—a normal hip and normal femur; top right—some partial dislocation (subluxation); bottom left—acetabulum (socket) is shallow and subluxation is present; bottom right—luxation (dislocation) is present, head of the femur is flattened.

parents of a prospective puppy are free of this disorder. The Orthopedic Foundation for Animals (OFA) has developed a widely accepted X-ray process that can often detect CHD. This test is generally used on dogs over the age of two, when the highest degree of certainty can be achieved. Another way of discovering CHD is through the Penn Hip test, which some experts consider an improvement over the X-ray process.

Giving Your Poodle Medicine

Knowing how to give your Poodle medicine is essential for all Poodle owners. You should be able to administer the prescription medicines your veterinarian recommends. Some dogs don't like medicine and will spit out pills and capsules.

One common way of getting a dog to take pills is to hide them inside some favorite treat. Another way is to fold the pill or capsule inside a little peanut butter on a small piece of bread.

A more direct way of administering pills is to open the Poodle's mouth, tilt its head back a little, and place the pill as far back on the dog's tongue as possible. Then simply close the dog's mouth, talk calmly to it, and wait for it to swallow.

Never throw the pill or capsule into the dog's mouth or tilt the animal's head back very far. These actions could cause the medicine to go into the windpipe instead of down the dog's throat.

Give liquid medicines in much the same way. Always take care not to tilt the head back too far, as this could cause strangling. Simply pour the medicine into the pocket formed in the corner of the mouth. Tilt the head back a short way, speak in slow, reassuring terms, and rub the underside of the Poodle's neck until you are certain it has swallowed the medicine.

Always follow your veterinarian's recommendations carefully about how much to administer and when, and about other factors that may relate to the specific medicine. Don't undo the good of a medicine by using more or less than is advised.

Health Areas to Watch

Accidents

If you have prepared adequately and taken the proper precautions to be a Poodle owner, you should be able to eliminate many potential accidents. But you cannot prevent them all, no

Handling Canine Emergencies

If you're fortunate, you and your Poodle will never have to go through a health emergency. If you do, much of what then happens to your pet depends on you. Here are some time-tested suggestions that may lessen the severity of any injuries to your Poodle or you.

• Keep calm. Don't do anything to let your Poodle pick up any anxiety you may be feeling.

• Convey to the hurt animal that you are here to make things right. Your Poodle will trust you and believe that the "Boss" will take away the pain.

• Even if the injured dog is your Toy Poodle and longtime pet, put a muzzle on the dog. Do it gently and reassuringly. If you don't have a muzzle, devise a makeshift one from a belt, leash, scarf, or tie.

• A severely injured dog, even a trusted Poodle, may be in shock or frantic. Don't you become an injured party too. Take every precaution to see that your dog doesn't further hurt itself, you, or some helpful friend.

• Once you have the dog securely muzzled, immediately attend to any bleeding.

• Be very careful as you attempt to move the Poodle. If at all possible, get someone to help you. Use a wide board, a small table, or whatever will serve as a secure stretcher. Don't handle the injured pet roughly or drop it after you have lifted it. Either action could do more damage.

• If you are alone you could use a jacket, a small throw rug, or even a tablecloth to make a slide to move the hurt animal. Be especially gentle and move very slowly.

• Call the veterinarian, or have someone else do so on your instructions. Let the clinic know the nature of the most obvious injuries and your estimated arrival time.

• Drive carefully to the veterinary clinic. Rough, fast driving could do more harm, and inattentive driving could put both you and your dog under medical care—or worse!

• In all your emergency actions, follow this sound medical injunction: "First, do no harm!"

matter how hard you try! Because you can't avert every mishap, you should try to be as ready as possible in case your Poodle is injured.

Heatstroke

One of the saddest and most unnecessary ways for a mature dog or puppy to die is from heatstroke. Many heatstrokes result from the dog's owner's ignorance or neglect. Most often this stupid and avoidable cause of death happens when a dog is left in a parked car on a sunny day when the outdoor temperature reaches 60°F (15.6°C) and above. The glass, metal, and insulation of the average automobile can make the vehicle the equivalent of a convection oven in only a few minutes.

Never leave a dog in a parked car in warm weather, even with the windows partially open. This holds even if you are just dashing into a store for a quick purchase; something could delay you and doom your pet to a miserable death.

Clinical signs of heatstroke include a dazed, shocked look, rapid and shallow breathing, a high fever, drooling, and gums that are bright red. Speed is crucial in this emergency. You must lower the dog's temperature as quickly as possible. To do so, pour cool water (mixed with rubbing alcohol if any is available) all over the dog's body. When the animal seems cooler, drive safely to the nearest veterinarian!

Bleeding

If your pet is bleeding, the first thing to do after taking safety precautions is to discover the source of the blood. When you are certain that you have found the right spot, apply firm but gentle pressure to the wound with your hand. If the bleeding is coming from a gash or cut on an extremity (legs or tail), apply a tourniquet between the injury and the dog's heart. Be careful to loosen this tourniquet every 15 minutes. Transport the bleeding pet to the veterinarian for further attention.

Poisons

Much of the time your Poodle is in your home, where it's likely that there are many items that can poison your pet—sometimes items you wouldn't even recognize as dangers! A number of things that can poison your Poodle are probably in your home right now, including those listed below.

• *Chocolate.* This American favorite can, in sufficient amounts, kill your Poodle. Don't give a dog chocolate, and put containers of the stuff out of reach of a curious dog.

• *Antifreeze.* Dogs seem to like the taste of this substance, but it can be a real killer. Don't neglect to clean up spills or leaks of this product, and always keep containers of antifreeze away from areas dogs frequent.

• *Various yard and garden plants.* Some of these can be fatal if a puppy or mature dog eats them. Landscaping favorites like azaleas, rhododendron, and even holly can bring about death. Wild plants such as mistletoe, poison

sumac, and poison ivy can be fatal as well. Check with your local county extension service for a list of poisonous plants, cultivated and wild, that grow near where you live. Avoid these plants with your dog.

• *Houseplants.* A few of the most common to guard against are poinsettia, jade, and dieffenbachia, which can cause fatalities in dogs that ingest parts of these or other plants. Contact a local nursery for a complete lineup of houseplants that are popular where your live and that could kill your dog.

• *Household cleaners and cleaning solvents, insecticides, pesticides, and fertilizers.* Any of these can do great harm to a Poodle should the dog come in close contact with them. Store all these and other household chemicals in safe places away from where you keep your Poodle. Clean up chemical spills promptly and thoroughly.

If your dog suddenly has convulsions, becomes listless or disoriented, or is unconscious, poison may be the culprit. Other clinical signs include a change in the color of the mucous membranes, vomiting, and diarrhea. Go immediately to the veterinary clinic with a Poodle exhibiting these signs.

Preventive Maintenance

Just as with any other thing of importance to you, your Poodle will require some preventive maintenance for it to stay in the best of shape. Some areas will require your attention throughout the life of the pet.

Teeth

Dogs depend on their teeth for many functions. Unless you pay close attention to its teeth, your dog will become unpleasant to be around,

Poodles are good chums. They enjoy other canines and especially humans for companionship.

prone to numerous oral problems, and may be in pain that could have been prevented. While your Poodle is still a young puppy, begin a regular regimen of good dental care. This usually includes taking your pet to the veterinarian twice a year. In addition, you can do a few things yourself to enhance your Poodle's dental health. Listed below are some recommendations.

• Regular inspections of your dog's teeth will reveal most problems and abnormalities. This chore can be done easily on a daily basis. Take a moment from play, training, or just being with your Poodle and look into its mouth.

• Look regularly (at least weekly) at the teeth, gums, throat, and outside areas around the mouth. You should seek tooth problems, stains on the teeth, and mouth sores. Also check for tartar, small foreign objects such as wood slivers, plant awns (bristles on the ends of some plants, such as grasses), or bone fragments that could have been picked up through gnawing or chewing.

• Be especially aware of tartar, which is not only unsightly but can also bring on gum disease or tooth problems.

• Start early with home cleaning of your Poodle's teeth. Just as with grooming, training, and other responsibilities of Poodle ownership, the earlier you establish an activity as a regular part of the dog's life, the easier it will be.

• To clean your Poodle's teeth, use veterinarian-approved brushes, utensils, and toothpaste designed for dogs, not for humans! Try brushing the teeth daily for best results, but never less than two or three times each week.

• Tartar scraping is an unpleasant chore that only gets worse if you neglect to do it. Consult your veterinarian about how often your Poodle will need your services as a tartar remover. Severe tartar buildup will probably require your veterinarian's skill.

• Many chew toys are designed to help stimulate the dog's gums and keep tartar to a minimum. However, although these items may assist you, no toy, biscuit, chew, or bone will do the job you can by looking after your dog's dental care regularly.

Eyes

Your Poodle's eyes are among its most beautiful assets, and eye care is another lifelong task you must assume when you decide to become a responsible dog owner. Poodles are active and can sometimes put themselves in danger of eye damage. You will need to become a canine risk manager to help your Poodle avoid potentially blinding injuries.

• Wherever you go with your Poodle or wherever your Poodle is allowed to go in your home, be proactive about removing sharp, eye-level things that could harm an exuberant dog's eyes. Your Poodle might not see the sharp wires, the rosebush thorns, or any other of the many things that could damage its eyes. You must try to make your pet's environment as safe as possible.

POODLE POINT

White (and other light-colored Poodles) will sometimes have dark stains around their eyes. Talk with your groomer and your veterinarian about the best kind of stain removers to use and the best way to use them.

• Caution children about throwing stones, playing with air rifles, or doing anything around your Poodle that could endanger its eyes.
• Protect your Poodle from chemical harm to its eyes. This includes avoiding fumes or residue that could get into the dog's eyes and irritate them.
• Never let your Poodle ride in the car with its head stuck out the window. It takes only a piece of road debris, or even a large insect, to hurt a pet's eyes at the highway speed of the average car.
• Check your dog's eyes daily for injuries, irritation, infection, foreign objects, or similar problems. The mucus that sometimes collects in the corner of a dog's eye is usually harmless and can be removed easily with a soft, slightly damp cloth. However, don't confuse this mucus with a discharge that could mean a problem.

Ears

Check your Poodle's ears as often as you should its teeth and eyes—daily! The inside parts of the Poodle's ears are not out in the open as they are in some other breeds. Take extra care to

This youngster is showing off what is known in Poodle circles as the puppy clip. This haircut is only for younger show dogs.

It is important when trimming your Poodle's nails to avoid hitting the vein in the toenail, commonly called the quick.

seek out and check this favorite hiding place for ear mites and ticks. Look for injuries and infections. Don't let small children put foreign objects in a dog's ears. Also, Poodles grow hair in their ears that must be plucked out before it mats and causes blockage and infection.

Feet and Toenails

In some places where Poodles live there is hard stone, concrete, or asphalt to wear down the dog's toenails as the animal runs. Although running under these conditions can keep the dog's nails worn down so they won't need much trimming, such hard surfaces can cause the dog bruises, abrasions, and wear to the pads of its feet. Salt and other chemicals found on city streets, parking lots, and sidewalks also can irritate or harm a dog's running gear.

A Poodle that spends most of its life indoors, maybe with access to a grassy backyard, will not have the footpad problems of an urban dog accustomed to running on paved roads. However, the nails of the indoor/backyard dog will not be worn down as an urban dog's would,

so you'll have to trim them. As with other aspects of grooming, the earlier such activities are introduced to the dog, the better.

You will need a good set of nail trimmers designed with dogs in mind. There are two kinds: the "scissor" type and the "guillotine" type. As your Poodle's nails grow, snip them back by trimming just the tips of each nail. Don't trim too much or you will hit the vein in the nail called the "quick," which may bleed. If you are unsure about how much nail is too much, use an emery board instead of nail clippers. You are less likely to injure the vein in the nail that way. After trimming, smooth the edges of the nail with an emery board or nail file. If you paint your Poodle's nails, be certain that the polish you use is safe in case the dog should gnaw off some of it.

As Your Poodle Grows Older

Poodles generally have long life spans, meaning that the adorable puppy you acquired when it was just a couple of months old may be with you for a decade and a half. If your Poodle was conceived in good genetic circumstances and then raised in a healthy environmental setting, your children should be able to grow up with that very dog. But how you care for the dog—taking on the responsibilities of feeding, exercising, training, and watching out for its overall health—will have an impact on the length and quality of its life.

Whatever you do, eventually the toddling puppy will make way for the bouncy adolescent, a canine "teenager" who will move in to allow the adult to take center stage. The adult will gradually age into a dignified, but still sprightly, senior. Seniority will begin well, but ever so gradually your beloved Poodle will slow down.

If dog shows hadn't been in existence, they would have been invented just so classy Poodles could be shown off.

As long as an old dog remains reasonably healthy, don't take away its little chores and duties, and try not to upset its routine. Don't be harsh with an oldster with slowed reflexes and bodily functions. Repay your Poodle in the same currency with which it has rewarded you all its life: love.

Euthanasia

Euthanasia is never an easy subject to plan for, discuss, or even contemplate, but there may come a time when your Poodle's existence is one of only pain and suffering. Your valiant old dog may have handled its aging process as bravely as possible, but age always wins. It will be up to you to see that your Poodle's losing fight against age isn't a prolonged and unnecessarily painful experience.

Unless your Poodle is killed in an accident, dies early of some ailment, or dies naturally, it will live a long life that will possibly leave you with one of the most difficult decisions a dog owner can ever have to make—that is, how much suffering is too much?

Barring an early death, one day your Poodle will look up at you in a questioning manner, wanting you to take the pains away, to make things good the way they used to be, to set things right. You have to make a tough adult decision here. Does this good dog, one that has loved you with all of its heart, deserve to stay alive in a pained or incapacitated state? Your veterinarian can help you with this decision and the timing of it. But only you can truly know when it is finally best to say good-bye.

Old dogs sleep a little more, play a little less, and still relish the quiet times near you and your family. The good care you gave the Poodle in earlier years will now start to pay extra dividends because of all the attention you've paid all along to the care of its nails, teeth, eyes, ears, and general health.

Your old Poodle will still show flashes of that spunky puppy you first came to love. It will still want to patrol its guard posts to make certain your household is secure. It will still need lots of tender, loving, care. Your Poodle may become a more frequent visitor at its veterinarian's office.

INFORMATION

Organizations
American Boarding Kennel Association
1702 E. Pikes Peak Avenue
Colorado Springs, CO 80909
Toll Free: 1-877-570-7788
Local: (719) 667-1600
Fax: (719) 667-0116
info@abka.com
(713) 668-1021

American Kennel Club
5580 Centerview Drive, Suite 200
Raleigh, NC 27606-3390
(919) 233-9767
akc.org

Canadian Kennel Club
89 Skyway Avenue, Suite 100
Etobicoke, Ontario
M9W 6R4
(416) 675-5511
information@ckc.ca

Poodle Club of America (PCA)
24922 Las Marias La
Mission Viejo, CA 92691
(949) 378-6701
poodleclubsecy@aol.com

Poodle Club of America
National RESCUE
The National Rescue Chairman
E-mail only: *poodleclubofamerica@yahoo.com*

Magazines
Dog Fancy
P.O. Box 53264
Boulder, CO 80322-3264
(303) 666-8504

Dog World
29 North Wacker Drive
Chicago, IL 60606-3298
(312) 726-2802

The Poodle Review
Holfin Publishing
4401 Zepher Street
Wheat Ridge, CO 80033

The Poodle Variety
P.O. Box 30430
Santa Barbara, CA 93130

Books
Alderton, David. *The Dog Care Manual.*
 Hauppauge, New York: Barron's Educational
 Series, Inc., 1986.
Baer, Ted. *Communicating with Your Dog.*
 Hauppauge, New York: Barron's Educational
 Series, Inc., 1989.
Brown, Robert M. *The Poodle Owner's Medical
 Manual.* Jackson, Wisconsin: Breed Manual
 Publications, 1987.
Dahl, Del. *The Complete Poodle.* New York, New
 York: Howell Book House, 1994.
Kalstone, Shirlee. *The Complete Poodle Clipping
 and Grooming Book.* New York, New York:
 Howell Book House, 1981.
Wrede, Barbara. *Civilizing Your Puppy.*
 Hauppauge, New York: Barron's Educational
 Series, Inc., 1992.

Further Reading on Poodles
Berenson, Laurien, *A Pedigree to Die For.* New
 York, New York: Kensington Publishing Corp.,
 1995.
Steinbeck, John, *Travels with Charley.* New York,
 New York: The Viking Press, Inc., 1962.

INDEX

About the Author

Joe Stahlkuppe, a lifelong dog fancier and breeder, writes dog columns for several pet and general interest publications. A former U.S. Army journalist in Vietnam and teacher, he is also the author of Barron's *Irish Setters: A Complete Pet Owner's Manual, Great Danes: A Complete Pet Owner's Manual, American Pit Bull and Staffordshire Terriers: A Complete Pet Owner's Manual,* and *Training Your Pit Bull.* Mr. Stahlkuppe lives with his wife, Cathie, on a small farm in Alabama.

Acknowledgments

I want to thank my wife, Cathie, my son, Shawn, and his wife, Lisa, and our four grandchildren—Catie, Peter, Julia, and Alexandra—for their patience with me during this endeavor. I want to thank all those tireless Poodle rescue organizations that do so much to rehome and adopt pets into better situations.

I also want to thank my talented editor, Annemarie McNamara, for her inestimable help in making this a better book. I would also like to acknowledge a parti-colored Poodle fan, Carla Lewis.

I most want to dedicate this book to those humans who have made Poodles an indispensable part of their lives.

Important Note

This pet owner's manual tells the reader how to buy or adopt, and care for a Poodle. The author and publisher consider it important to point out that the advice given in the book is meant primarily for normally developed dogs of excellent physical health and sound temperament.

Anyone who acquires a fully grown dog should be aware that the animal has already formed its basic impressions of human beings. The new owner should observe the animal carefully, including its behavior toward humans, and, whenever possible, should meet the previous owner.

Caution is further advised in the association of children with dogs, in meeting with other dogs, and in exercising the dog without a leash.

Even well-behaved and carefully supervised dogs can sometimes damage property or cause accidents. It is therefore in the owner's interest to be adequately insured against such eventualities, and we strongly urge all dog owners to purchase a liability policy that also covers their dog.

Photo Credits

Norvia Behling: 18, 23, 24 (top), 25, 28, 35, 37, 41, 45 (top), 61, and 89; Kent Dannen: 16 (right), and 55; Tara Darling: 5, 7, 22, 36, 58, 60, 62, 68, 77, 90, and 92; Cheryl Ertelt: 2–3, 12, 31 (left), 42, 48, 72, and 73 (top); Isabelle Francais: 4, 8, 9, 13, 16 (left), 17, 19, 20, 24 (bottom), 31 (right), 32, 38, 39, 43, 49, 50, 51, 52, 57, 59, 63, 69, 71, 73 (bottom), 74, 75, 78, 80, and 83; Pets by Paulette: 11, 21, 29, 33, 34, 44, 45 (bottom), 56, 66, 76, and 85; Connie Summers: 14, 53, and 54.

Cover Photos

Pets by Paulette: front cover; Norvia Behling: back cover; Tara Darling: inside front cover; Cheryl Ertelt: inside back cover.

All inquiries should be addressed to:
Barron's Educational Series, Inc.
250 Wireless Boulevard
Hauppauge, NY 11788
www.barronseduc.com

ISBN-13: 978-0-7641-3666-5
ISBN-10: 0-7641-3666-6

Library of Congress Catalog Card No. 2006032083

Library of Congress Cataloging-in-Publication Data
Stahlkuppe, Joe.
 Poodles : everything about purchase, care, nutrition, behavior, and training / Joe Stahlkuppe ; illustrations by Michele Earle Bridges.
  p. cm. — (A complete pet owner's manual)
 Includes index.
 ISBN-13: 978-0-7641-3666-5
 ISBN-10: 0-7641-3666-6
 1. Poodles. I. Title.

SF429.P85S67 2007
636.72'8—dc22   2006032083

Printed in China
9 8 7 6 5 4